T0304446

Creating Images Using AI

Creating Images Using AI: A Step-by-Step Guide to Midjourney is an essential resource for professionals and others looking to harness the amazing power of AI-powered image generator programs and to ensure they keep up to date with developments in this rapidly evolving field. This comprehensive guide offers an in-depth exploration of Midjourney, one of the most respected programs available today, used by over 17 million users.

The book covers the fundamentals of setting up and using Midjourney through to advanced techniques for crafting precise text- and image-based prompts to ensure high-quality images. Detailed step-by-step instructions are provided to facilitate a thorough understanding of the program, supported throughout by screenshots and examples of Midjourney image output. Included are case studies of talented artists who use Midjourney as a creative tool, with examples of their inspiring art to motivate readers. A dedicated chapter offers resources for photographers, designers, and artists to expand their skills, and to stay up to date with the latest developments in AI technology.

Whether you're seeking to enhance your professional toolkit or simply explore AI as a creative outlet, this book offers the knowledge and skills to harness Midjourney's full potential. For professionals in photography, graphic design, marketing, advertising, and education, it provides the essential tools to stay ahead in a rapidly changing industry.

Julie Pallant (PhD) is a photographer/digital artist who makes extensive use of artificial intelligence (AI) in creating her artwork and provides an AI training and consultancy service. She has 25 years' experience as a university lecturer teaching and developing training material on psychology and statistics, including an internationally best-selling statistical computing textbook currently in its 7th edition.

"Creating Images Using AI: A Step-by-Step Guide to Midjourney by Julie Pallant brilliantly bridges the gap between traditional photography and the innovative world of Midjourney. Packed with practical tips and stunning examples, it's the ultimate resource for anyone looking to elevate their craft and embrace new creative possibilities."

Simon Hunter, Photographer, former Professor of Applied Linguistics

"Julie Pallant's book *Creating Images Using AI: A Step-by-Step Guide to Midjourney* is an indispensable tool for creative professionals needing to adapt to the rapidly evolving world of AI image generation. It provides a comprehensive, clear, and thorough guide to the Midjourney program, including detailed practical examples of its many and varied applications."

Mark Kratochvil, Lecturer, Diploma of Photography and Photo Imaging, Torrens University, Australia

"Julie Pallant's book, *Creating Images Using AI: A Step-by-Step Guide to Midjourney*, is an invaluable resource for anyone looking to explore the capabilities of AI in image generation and hone their prompting skills. Whether for personal projects or professional endeavors, this book offers clear, practical insights that will help you create stunning visuals with ease."

Ayesha Hilton, Author, Creator, Entrepreneur

Creating Images Using AI
A Step-by-Step Guide to Midjourney

Julie Pallant

CRC Press
Taylor & Francis Group
Boca Raton London New York

CRC Press is an imprint of the
Taylor & Francis Group, an **informa** business

Designed cover image: Cover Image by Julie Pallant

First edition published 2025
by CRC Press
2385 NW Executive Center Drive, Suite 320, Boca Raton FL 33431

and by CRC Press
4 Park Square, Milton Park, Abingdon, Oxon, OX14 4RN

CRC Press is an imprint of Taylor & Francis Group, LLC

© 2025 Taylor & Francis Group, LLC

First edition published by CRC 2025

ISBN: 9781032891996 (hbk)
ISBN: 9781032886725 (pbk)
ISBN: 9781003541677 (ebk)

DOI: 10.1201/9781003541677

Typeset in Palatino
by Newgen Publishing UK

Contents

Contents

Acknowledgments

A big thank you to everyone who has helped me in the creation of this book. I am grateful to the AI artists who agreed to be featured in the book and who provided images and background information about their AI creations: Damien Bredberg, Ayesha Hilton, Dirk Fleischmann, Jade Jenerai, Okki Peace Kim, and Salome Castro.

Thanks also go to those who agreed to be interviewed about their views on AI: Patrick Rodriguez, William Aung, Damien Bredberg, and Simon Hunter. I am grateful for the positive feedback provided by Ayesha Hilton, Simon Hunter, and Mark Kratochvil in their endorsements.

A special thanks to Simon Hunter for his encouragement and feedback throughout the process of writing the book and preparing it for publication.

Finally, and most importantly, an enormous thank you to my husband for his unwavering support and for all the extra housework, cooking, shopping, etc. that he has had to do while I was locked away in my study!

Website

Given the rapid growth of AI, image-generating programs are changing all the time. This is particularly true for Midjourney which regularly brings out new versions, incorporating new features.

To keep updated with changes to the program visit the website that was set up to accompany this book. You can access it using this link: https://linktr.ee/juliepallant

Videos demonstrating some of the techniques described in the book are included for those of you that like to learn by watching, rather than reading.

1

Introduction

The AI Revolution

What an exciting time in history to be alive! The pace at which the world is evolving is unprecedented, driven by advancements in technology and artificial intelligence (AI) in particular. This AI revolution is reshaping industries, altering job markets, and redefining how we interact with the world around us. The rapid development and integration of AI into our daily lives can be both exhilarating and unsettling. It presents a future filled with possibilities as well as challenges.

Today, AI is integrated into everyday technology; it is in our homes, our phones, and our computers. Online, it enhances user experiences and streamlines operations in fields such as health care, where it aids in diagnosis and treatment plans; finance through personalized investment strategies; and the creative industries by enabling the generation of images, art, and music.

One of the biggest AI advancements we have seen over the past few years is the development of AI image generation programs where it is possible to produce images just by providing a written description. Although a novelty at first, the world of AI image generation has exploded with many millions of people creating or using AI images every day.

AI image generation is set to have a significant impact on a variety of industries, revolutionizing the way we create and interact with visual content. Among the industries poised for the most dramatic changes are photography, advertising, graphic design, art, business, entertainment, and education. In response to these AI-driven changes, the need for adaptability has never been more critical. Traditional roles are being transformed, requiring individuals to acquire new skills and adapt to new ways of working. The skills and knowledge that served us in the past may not suffice for the challenges and opportunities of tomorrow.

To navigate this shifting world, we must be willing to learn and acquire new skills continually. Staying informed and adaptable is not just advantageous – it's essential for anyone looking to thrive in a future that remains undefined. Embracing change and the learning it demands is the only way to ensure we do not fall behind as the world moves forward.

Aim of This Book

My goal in writing this book on the Midjourney program is to provide you with the knowledge and skills to take full advantage of all the opportunities that AI image generation has to offer now and into the future. For some of you, this might mean integrating AI into your current workflow, helping you to do your job

DOI: 10.1201/9781003541677-1

more creatively and efficiently. For others, this may provide you with a skill base to reinvent yourself in response to the inevitable job losses and restructuring that are already impacting many creative industries.

The ability of AI image generators to create images quickly and easily is not just applicable as a work-related tool. For many millions of people across the world it is a fun and enjoyable way to express their creativity. This is how I started using Midjourney – just to have fun creating the images that I had never been able to achieve through my less-than-successful attempts at watercolor, drawing, and painting.

Whatever the reason behind your desire to learn image generation using Midjourney, this book is designed for you. It takes you step by step through the process of generating high-quality images using the Midjourney program. I do this in an easy to follow, non-technical way that is designed to teach you the necessary skills and build your confidence. It is suitable for both complete beginners and those of you who have had some experience with the Midjourney program but want to ensure that you get the most out of its many features.

At the time of writing this book (June 2024) there are a growing number of programs that offer AI for generating images and text. Navigating this world of choice can be overwhelming and confusing when you are first dipping your toe tentatively into the world of AI. Instagram, Facebook, and YouTube are full of competing claims about which AI program offers the best creations.

To prevent confusion and limit the possibility of your brain exploding, I have decided to focus this book on just one of the image-generating AI programs: Midjourney. According to many reviewers, it is currently the leading program in the field. As of November 1, 2023, Midjourney had over 16 million users (Broz, 2023). The program is incredibly adaptable, producing quality images in a wide variety of mediums, including photography, line drawings, cartoons, illustrations, logos, or comics; replicating the effect of using acrylic, oil paint, alcohol ink, or stained glass. It can produce images that are abstract or realistic, detailed or minimalistic, in the style of the traditional art masters, or modern graffiti and any combination of the above.

To get the most out of Midjourney, and indeed any image generator, it is important that you understand how to communicate with the AI computer models. A new term has been coined to describe this skill: "Promptology".

> As AI systems continue to evolve and their integration into everyday life deepens, a solid understanding of Promptology will become increasingly indispensable. Not just for technologists, AI researchers, and developers, but for anyone looking to tap into the transformative power of AI.
>
> *Olla, 2023*

FIGURE 1.1
Prompt: image of a woman talking to an AI robot, they are standing face to face with both looking closely to each other's face listening closely to what is being said.

Throughout the book, I include clear instructions, tips, and hints on how to write good prompts and refine them, when necessary, to achieve the best images possible. I provide a wide variety of images as examples, along with the prompts used to generate them, so you can try them out yourself. I list resources that you may wish to use to expand your understanding of the Midjourney program and to keep up to date with developments.

The book is designed to be applicable across a wide range of different professions and industries that either create or utilize images. The examples used throughout the book are chosen to be relevant to photographers, graphic designers, artists, designers, content creators, and educators.

Midjourney is also a powerful tool for those of us who create images for personal enjoyment. According to a recent review of Midjourney users, up to 83% reported using the program as a form of art therapy and mood enhancer: "it makes you feel better, de-stress and forget about time for a while – it benefits the body and the mind" (Krivec, 2023).

I hope that this book will not only give you the skills to use Midjourney effectively but also inspire you to consider the many ways that images generated by the program can be used. In the final chapter, I provide a number of case studies of early adopters of AI image generation who have made very effective use of Midjourney, integrating it successfully into their creative work, both professionally and personally. These examples are designed to inspire you to consider how you too may be able to make the most of what AI image generation offers to take your creativity to the next level.

Who Is This Book For?

When I wrote this book, I had two groups of people in mind:

a. those of you who need to create images for your work (content creators, website designers, photographers, artists, and graphic designers) and
b. anyone who wants to explore their creativity and bring a bit of beauty into the world.

I have written it in a practical, non-technical style, assuming no prior knowledge of AI or computer programming. The aim is to get you up and running as quickly, and as painlessly, as possible. You might be pleasantly surprised by just how fast and easy it is to start producing stunning images.

The rise of Artificial Intelligence (AI) has created quite an emotional response throughout the creative community. Many millions of people worldwide have welcomed the arrival of AI programs with excitement, using rapidly evolving tools to enhance their creative processes and assist with routine tasks.

For some creatives, however, the rise of AI and the explosion of publicity surrounding it has generated feelings of fear, confusion, distrust, and loss of confidence. Many fear that they might lose their jobs if they don't keep up with the latest AI developments, adding to their sense of insecurity. A common response to feeling overwhelmed is to stick your head in the sand and avoid any discussion of the topic, hoping that AI will be a short-term fad that will go away.

As a psychologist, I can understand these emotional reactions, particularly given the very rapid pace of technological change and the uncertainty it brings. Change can be difficult to face, particularly when it appears it could threaten both our jobs and our identities. In writing this book, I aim to make navigating this change process as painless as possible and to help you discover just how amazing these AI tools are.

It is important to remember that AI is not here to replace humans but rather to augment their capabilities. AI tools can help automate repetitive tasks, analyze data, and generate personalized designs, freeing up time for more creative aspects of your work. AI can enhance efficiency and productivity, but it is not a replacement for human creativity and ingenuity.

We all must accept the fact that AI is here to stay and will continue to play an increasingly important role in society generally and the creative world more specifically. By embracing AI and learning how to use it effectively, you can stay ahead of the curve and produce creative and innovative material.

Outline of the Book

I had three main goals in mind when writing this book.

First, I wanted to introduce you (gently) to this new world of artificial intelligence, the image generation programs that are available, and to demonstrate some of the ways that AI might be used in different discipline areas. This is the focus of Chapters 1–4.

The second goal was to offer an easy-to-follow guide to Midjourney that ensured you were able to make the most of its many features with the least amount of stress. These instructions are provided in Chapters 5 and 6.

The third goal was to inspire you with additional resources and examples of how other artists are using Midjourney as a powerful creative tool. These can be found in Chapters 7 and 8.

I have provided details about the content of each of the eight chapters as follows:

Chapter 1: Introduction

This chapter provides a brief introduction to the book, explaining why it is important that professionals develop skills in using AI image generation and explaining who it is for and what is covered. I describe how I came to be interested in Midjourney, a bit about my background, and why I wrote the book. This is intended to set the scene and encourage you to make an effort to embrace AI and learn what Midjourney has to offer.

Chapter 2: AI: What Is It and What Impact Will It Have?

In Chapter 2, I provide a very brief and non-technical introduction to AI. I focus on the positive and negative impacts of AI and the ethical, legal, and copyright issues that you need to be aware of. My intention is to provide just enough background information for you to understand AI but not too much that it is overwhelming.

Chapter 3: Creative Uses for AI Image Generators

In this chapter, I highlight a range of different applications of AI for photographers, graphic designers, artists, marketers, and other creative professionals. I aim to demonstrate how applicable AI is across a wide range of different disciplines and professions. I include many images generated by Midjourney to show its versatility and the quality and creativity of the images that are possible.

Chapter 4: AI Image-Generating Programs

In this chapter, I provide an overview of the range of AI image-generating programs, both free and paid. I introduce you to the Midjourney program and explain why I (and many others) believe that Midjourney is the best program currently available in terms of ease of use and image quality.

Chapter 5: Getting Started with Midjourney

The focus of Chapter 5 is the Midjourney program, where I will take you step by step through the basics of using the program to create images. It explores the various features of the interface and the steps involved in generating, refining, and exporting images. I demonstrate how the images can be organized into folders and how to use filters to find specific images. I also show how you can explore the images that are generated by other members of the Midjourney community and learn from these examples.

Chapter 6: Writing Good Prompts

Chapter 6 extends the knowledge and skills covered in Chapter 5 and provides you with a more detailed understanding of how to write effective prompts to ensure you obtain the images that you want. I cover a number of more advanced techniques that allow you to refine your prompts. I also demonstrate how to use images as part of your prompt to show Midjourney the type of result that you require.

Chapter 7: Further Inspiration

In Chapter 7, I provide some inspiring case studies of creatives who have embraced the use of AI tools to improve their creativity and efficiency. This includes examples of their work and extracts from interviews I conducted that explored how they feel about AI, their views on its impact, and how they utilize it as part of their professional and personal lives. Examples of AI artists who use their art to raise awareness of social and environmental issues are included to show the many and varied ways that AI images are being utilized. For those of you looking for ways to make money, I describe some of the ways that you can "monetize" your art and suggest two YouTube channels that you might find helpful for exploring possible business opportunities.

Chapter 8: Additional Resources

A range of additional resources are provided in Chapter 8 to ensure you make the most of Midjourney and fully benefit from what it offers in terms of image generation. This includes online resources, links, and social media sites for users who wish to stay up to date with developments and share their work. I describe two additional programs that you can use to enhance your Midjourney images – Adobe Photoshop to edit your images and Topaz Gigapixel AI to enlarge your images for printing. I include detailed examples of how I have used Photoshop to edit, refine, and manipulate my own Midjourney images.

Chapter 9: Conclusion

In this final chapter, I review the main topics covered in the book and encourage you to dive in, play with Midjourney, experiment with prompts, and see what you get. Be warned – it can be addictive!

Who Am I and Why Did I Write This Book?

I first discovered Midjourney back in December 2022 and fell in love with the idea that I could create images just by describing what I wanted in words. Although the images it produced at that time were very primitive compared to its current creations, I could see its enormous potential to improve the creativity and efficiency of my work as both a photographer and digital artist. On a more personal level, I confess that I really enjoyed using Midjourney as a form of art therapy – a creative escape from the real world!

As my skills in persuading Midjourney to produce interesting, quirky images improved, I found I was able to produce images to sell that proved very popular as cards and prints at my market stall. My AI-image-generated images attracted a lot of curiosity and interest from other photographers, artists, graphic designers, book authors, and content creators who were keen to learn more about it. This led to me producing instructional materials to use as part of a training and consultancy service I provided to other creatives in my local area. It was from these initial training notes that the idea of this current book emerged.

In writing this book, I have drawn on the knowledge and skills I have developed from my 25 years' experience as a university lecturer, my background as an Educational and Counselling Psychologist, my experience as an author of an internationally best-selling textbook, and more recently as a photographer and digital artist using Midjourney as part of my work.

Seven years ago, I retired as an Associate Professor, Director of Research and Graduate Studies at the University of Melbourne, Australia, where I taught a range of subjects, including psychology, research skills, and statistics. I also ran my own training and consulting service and was fortunate to travel the world running workshops teaching people how to use a variety of different computing software packages. My workshops were very popular in large part because of the clear, well-structured approach that I took to teaching, which made even quite complex concepts understandable for both students and professionals alike.

As an Educational Psychologist and lecturer, I have spent my career exploring how people learn and how to facilitate effective learning experiences. In writing this book, I have drawn on this expertise to create a guide that uses a logical, structured approach to learning Midjourney, breaks down complex concepts into clear, concise language, and anticipates common areas of confusion that you may encounter. I use practical examples throughout the book to make the material more meaningful and relevant.

This Midjourney guide is modeled on my best-selling textbook, *SPSS Survival Manual: A Step-by-Step Guide to Data Analysis using SPSS*, which was first published in 2001 and is now in its 7th edition. In my SPSS book, I lead the reader step by step through the process of learning the statistical computing package SPSS, an approach that has proved very popular. Using the same easy-to-follow style, I have carefully crafted the instructions, and the screen captures that I provide in this Midjourney book to ensure that each step is clear. I ensure you have a good grasp of the basic skills required before moving on to more advanced options.

The other set of skills that I have drawn on in the creation of this book is my experience as a photographer and digital artist, a business that I set up 7 years ago following my retirement from academia. My photography work, which is primarily focused on headshots, portraits, and creative composite portraiture, was one of the main reasons that I was attracted to exploring the potential of AI-assisted image generation tools. In addition to using AI in my photography work, I also produce and sell a range of products with AI-generated images, including prints, canvases, cards, mugs, coasters, cushions, and books, which are sold through local galleries, markets, and online marketplaces.

For the past 2 years, I have been a regular columnist for the *Better Photography Magazine* (Australian edition), where I publish instructional guides on Adobe Lightroom and Photoshop. The last four articles featured guides to using AI-assisted tools that have been incorporated into these programs making the process of photo-editing and retouching so much easier.

I am excited to share my knowledge and experience with you in this book as I am passionate about making AI image generation accessible to everyone. With the right guidance, I believe anyone can become skilled in the use of Midjourney to produce good quality, creative images. I hope to inspire you to explore the many creative possibilities of Midjourney.

Website

Given the rapid growth of AI, image-generating programs are changing all the time. This is particularly true for Midjourney, which regularly brings out new versions, incorporating new features. As you read through the instructions provided in Chapters 5 and 6 some of the screenshots of the program may not exactly match what you see on your screen.

To keep you updated on changes to the program, I have set up a website to accompany this book. You can access it using the link below:

Access to the book's website: https://linktr.ee/juliepallant

I will also be adding videos demonstrating some of the techniques described in the book for those of you who like to learn by watching rather than reading.

References

Broz, M. (2023, November 2). Midjourney statistics. *Photutorial*. https://phototutorial.com/midjourney-statistics

Krivec, R. (2023, September 14). Midjourney statistics (how many people use Midjourney). *Colorlib*. https://colorlib.com/wp/midjourney-statistics/#h-how-many-people-use-midjourney

Olla, P. (2023, July 21). Promptology: The future of AI interaction unveiled. *Medium*. https://medium.com/@phillip.olla/promptology-the-future-of-ai-interaction-unveiled-d619e8ceb3d4

2

AI: What Is It and What Impact Will It Have?

Introduction

In this book, I am not going to give you a complex, detailed explanation of AI and all the technology behind it. I know most of you wouldn't read it anyway! This chapter provides a quick overview of AI technology, just to give you some background understanding. You do not need to have a technical background to use AI, but it does help if you grasp the basics of the process involved behind the scenes.

One of the other important issues to understand when using AI image-generated art, particularly if you intend to use the images commercially, is the legal, ethical, and moral concerns that have been raised. Serious concerns have been raised about the rights of the artists whose artworks have been included in the data used to train the AI data, the possible infringement of copyright, and privacy concerns about the AI's ability to produce realistic images of individuals without their consent, and the implications for society as it becomes more difficult to distinguish between reality and fake images.

What Is AI?

Although it has been described as a revolution, the rise of AI from a theoretical concept to a practical tool reflects decades of research and development behind the scenes. Early achievements in AI include the development of algorithms that enabled computers to perform tasks that typically require human intelligence, such as playing chess and understanding spoken language.

AI is essentially about creating machines that can mimic a human's ability to learn, understand, and make decisions. The core of AI lies in "algorithms", which are sets of instructions that computers follow to perform tasks. These tasks could range from simple ones, like calculating sums, to more complex ones, like identifying patterns in data or even recognizing faces in photographs.

Machine learning is particularly powerful because it allows AI systems to improve over time. As they are exposed to more data, their ability to make accurate predictions or decisions gets better. This aspect of

DOI: 10.1201/9781003541677-2

AI is incredibly beneficial in creative fields such as photography and art, where nuances and details can significantly impact the final output.

A more advanced form of machine learning is deep learning, which utilizes structures called neural networks. These networks are inspired by the human brain and are particularly effective at processing and learning from large amounts of complex data. In the disciplines of photography and art, deep learning has been instrumental in advancements like enhancing image resolution, colorizing black and white photos, and even creating entirely new artistic images.

The AI computers are fed data in the form of millions of images harvested from the internet, social media, stock image libraries etc. The machines are taught what each of the images represent and over time their ability to distinguish, for example, the features of a dog and a cat, improve. So, when we request an image of a cat the AI image generator understands the ingredients that make up a cat and can produce one for us.

It is important to note that the computer is not copying an existing image of a cat that it has in its database. It creates one from scratch using the information that it has learned about what a cat looks like. This makes it much more flexible than using a stock image library approach of giving you an image that exists.

We can ask for an image that includes characteristics that would not be present in any of the existing cat images on which the computer was trained. For example, we could ask for a black cat with a unicorn horn, and it would produce one for us (see Figure 2.1).

Prompt: Photograph of a black cat with a unicorn horn

FIGURE 2.1
Image obtained from Midjourney using the prompt: photograph of a black cat with a unicorn horn.

Each time we generate an image using a prompt, we get a unique image that has been manufactured on the spot for us. Even if we were to use exactly the same prompt again, we would get a different image. If we copy a prompt from someone else's image we find on the Midjourney site and run this ourselves, we do not get the same image – sometimes the results are dramatically different!

To illustrate this point, I generated a second image using the same prompt, but it resulted in a different cat with a different background (see Figure 2.2). The unicorn horn was very similar – I suspect that the program had not been trained on many examples of unicorn horns to learn from!

Prompt: Photograph of a black cat with a unicorn horn

FIGURE 2.2
Image obtained from Midjourney using the same prompt as in Figure 2.1.

What Are the Likely Impacts of AI?

Reactions to AI have been mixed. While some commentators are screaming that it is the end of the world as we know it, others have welcomed it with open arms. Whether we like it or not, AI is here to stay, and it is important for us to keep up to date with developments so that we respond appropriately.

I have been keeping my ear to the ground, trying to understand what the future holds for those of us working as photographers, graphic designers, artists, and related fields. In keeping with the AI theme of this book, I also asked for help from ChatGPT (an AI text generator program) to summarize both the positive and negative aspects of AI for us creatives. (I have edited its response for clarity and to remove some of the highly emotive words that ChatGPT tends to use.)

The Positive Impacts of AI Image Generation

- **Enhanced Creativity and Inspiration**: AI image generators can serve as powerful tools for sparking creativity. They allow artists and designers to explore new visual styles and ideas that may not have been easily accessible or even conceivable before. For instance, a graphic designer can use AI to quickly generate a range of visual concepts, helping to jump-start the creative process.
- **Efficiency and Time Saving**: For professionals working under tight deadlines, AI image generators can be a lifesaver. These tools can rapidly produce high-quality images, layouts, or mock-ups, significantly reducing the time spent on initial drafts and allowing more focus on refinement and customization.
- **Accessibility and Democratization**: AI tools have made advanced artistic capabilities more accessible to a wider audience. This democratization means that individuals and small businesses without large budgets can produce professional-level visuals, leveling the playing field in the creative industry.
- **Aid in Learning and Experimentation**: For those learning the ropes of graphic design or photography, AI image generators can serve as educational tools, providing a hands-on way to understand composition, color theory, and other design principles.

Negative Impacts or Areas of Concern

- **Potential for Job Displacement**: One of the biggest concerns is that AI image generators might reduce the demand for human artists and designers. As AI becomes more capable of producing sophisticated and diverse artworks, there is a fear that this could lead to job displacement, particularly in fields, such as photography, art, and graphic design.
- **Issues of Originality and Authenticity**: AI-generated images raise questions about originality. Since these tools often rely on vast databases of existing artwork to create new images, it can lead to debates over the authenticity of AI-generated art and whether it can truly be considered "original".
- **Over-Reliance and Stifled Creativity**: There's a risk that over-reliance on AI tools might lead to a homogenization of design and a reduction in the development of personal style and creativity. Artists and designers might find themselves leaning too heavily on AI-generated suggestions, potentially stifling their own unique creative voice.
- **Ethical and Legal Considerations**: The use of AI in art and design brings up various ethical and legal issues, including copyright infringement and the ethical implications of using AI to replicate the styles of specific artists. Navigating these challenges will be crucial as AI tools become more prevalent.

One of the key areas of concern in relation to AI image generation is the ethical and legal implications – I expand on this in more detail in the next section.

Ethical, Legal, and Moral Issues

While AI image generation has opened up a world of creative opportunities, it also raises a number of ethical, legal, and moral challenges that you need to be aware of. I have addressed some of these below.

Copyright and Attribution

AI models trained on vast datasets often "scrape" images from the internet without proper attribution to artists. This raises questions about the rights of creators whose work inadvertently becomes part of the training data. Artists are not currently given the right to "opt out" of having their work used in this way. AI images may infringe on the original creators' intellectual property rights, as the AI might create new works that closely resemble existing copyrighted material. Unfortunately, the person creating the AI art may not be aware of this at the time, and it may result in legal action in the future. Balancing the rights of artists with the advancement of AI creativity is crucial but challenging.

Content Quality and Misinformation

AI-generated content can sometimes be misleading or of poor quality, resulting in misinformation, biased narratives, and harmful stereotypes. As AI-generated content develops it will become harder to distinguish between reality and AI-created works. Consumers may unknowingly encounter AI images of famous people and believe what they see is true. For example, an image of Pope Francis wearing a stylish white puffer jacket was widely circulated on the internet, showcasing how AI can fabricate scenarios that attract widespread attention. Another example was the AI images depicting Donald Trump's arrest, which were circulated widely enough to blur the lines between reality and AI-generated fiction for many viewers.

Biases and Representation

Depending on the data sources that an AI model is trained on, it may inherit biases and stereotypes that it will then go on to perpetuate. This issue is prevalent in various forms, such as cultural, racial, and gender biases, significantly impacting society by perpetuating existing inequalities.

One example of how AI image generators can reflect existing gender biases is seen in the field of STEM (Science, Technology, Engineering, and Mathematics). A study conducted by the UNDP Accelerator Lab (Nikolic & Jovicic, 2023) tested popular AI image generators DALL-E 2 and Stable Diffusion, by asking them to generate images representing professions like engineers, scientists, mathematicians, and IT experts. The results overwhelmingly depicted men, reinforcing the stereotype of STEM fields as male-dominated, despite women making up a significant percentage of graduates in these fields globally.

This study not only illustrates how AI can perpetuate gender stereotypes, but also highlights the risk of discouraging women from pursuing careers in STEM by failing to represent them in these roles adequately. If you would like to read the full article on this study, details of the article and web link are provided in the reference section at the end of this chapter.

The issue of AI bias is a topic of concern for large corporations such as IBM. In a recent article on their website, they address this issue and outline how companies can recognize and address the damaging impact of AI bias (IBM Data and AI Team, 2023).

Privacy and Consent

AI image generators can produce realistic images of individuals without their consent, raising privacy concerns. There is the risk of misuse, such as creating unauthorized or harmful content featuring someone's likeness. The issue extends to the use of publicly available images to train AI models, which might include personal photos shared online.

Beyond individual concerns, the ease with which AI can generate believable images poses broader societal questions about the nature of truth and trust in the digital world. The potential for creating indistinguishable fake images can undermine public trust in media and information, contributing to the spread of misinformation.

Ownership of AI Images

Ownership in relation to AI image generation is an issue which is still to be resolved. As AI creates images based on existing artworks or photographs, questions arise about who owns the rights to these new creations. Copyright law traditionally protects works created by human authors. However, AI-generated images do not have inherent rights under copyright law.

Currently, there is no legal recognition of AI as an author or creator. Therefore, AI-generated works are not automatically protected by copyright. "If an AI-generated artwork is not protected by copyright, it belongs to the public domain. Anyone can freely use, copy, distribute or use it for commercial purposes" (Matulionyte, 2019).

Impact on Employment and Creativity

As AI algorithms become more adept at generating art, music, and visual content, there is a risk that many will lose their jobs and whole industries will collapse. This clearly has consequences for both individuals and society as a whole. There may need to be changes to the labor laws and employment contracts to account for AI's role in creative industries. Balancing technological progress with preserving human creativity and expression will be an ongoing practical, legal, ethical, and moral challenge. There are no easy answers to addressing these issues – a collaborative effort involving creatives, employers, policymakers, and society at large will be required to balance the needs of all involved.

What Can We Do to Create and Use AI Images Ethically?

There are a few things we can do to ensure we are creating and using AI images ethically. Remember that AI-generated art is a blend of human creativity and machine learning. Responsible use of AI as a tool ensures that both artists and viewers benefit from this exciting intersection of art and technology.

- When sharing AI-generated art, make it clear that it was created by an AI algorithm. Transparency helps viewers understand the process and appreciate the role of technology.
- If the prompt was based on a specific artist's style, acknowledge their influence. Mentioning the artists whose work contributed to the prompt shows respect for their creativity.
- If you share or display AI-generated art, provide proper attribution to the original human prompt creators. Even though the art was generated by an algorithm, the prompt was crafted by human artists.
- Not all AI-generated art is equally impressive or meaningful. Assess the pieces that you share, emphasizing quality, and uniqueness. Flooding social media with low-quality AI art can dilute its impact. Choose wisely and share selectively.
- Be alert to the possibility of biases, stereotypes, or discrimination that may be present in the images you create and present.
- Encourage AI artists to explore diverse themes and styles. Celebrate art that challenges norms and represents a wide range of perspectives.
- If AI-generated art includes recognizable faces or personal information, obtain consent before sharing it publicly. Privacy rights matter even in the digital realm.
- Ensure that the art does not harm individuals or communities. Be cautious about sensitive topics and avoid offensive content.
- Use AI-generated art as an opportunity to educate others about the technology behind it. Explain how AI models work and the role of data in shaping their output. Engage in discussions about AI art, its impact, and its place in the art world. Foster curiosity and critical thinking.

References

IBM Data and AI team (2023, October 16). Shedding light on AI bias with real world examples. *Think 2024*. www.ibm.com/blog/shedding-light-on-ai-bias-with-real-world-examples

Matulionyte, R. (2019). AI-generated art: who owns the copyright. *The Lighthouse*. https://lighthouse.mq.edu.au/article/december-2019/AI-generated-art-who-owns-the-copyright

Nikolic, K. & Jovicic, J. (2023, April 3). Reproducing inequality: How AI image generators show biases against women in STEM. *United Nations Development Program*. www.undp.org/serbia/blog/reproducing-inequality-how-ai-image-generators-show-biases-against-women-stem

3

Creative Uses for AI Image Generators

Introduction

This chapter is dedicated to helping you understand and harness the power of AI in image creation, whether you are a photographer, a digital artist, or a content creator. There is an immense range of styles, mediums, and formats that are possible, just by describing what you want. Sometimes it can be fun to let Midjourney generate ideas. I am constantly amazed at the creativity of Midjourney to produce images that I could not have imagined.

The images generated using AI tools can be used in a wide variety of ways – as finished artwork, modified to create composite works, or as inspiration for the creation of works using more traditional mediums. I will explore some of these applications to whet your appetite.

Digital Artists/Graphic Designers

Image generator programs have been a godsend for many digital artists, helping them produce work in a fraction of the time compared with more traditional mediums. Many entrepreneurial AI artists are using images generated in Midjourney to create products that are earning them hundreds of thousands of dollars in passive income (allegedly). Print-on-demand services (e.g. Printify, Printful, and Gelato) are used which create the product featuring the Midjourney image and send it directly to the customer.

There are millions of products to choose from, including greeting cards, phone cases, stationery, stickers, candles, mugs, wall art, clothing, bed linen, and other household products. These are then sold on platforms such as Etsy or Shopify at a profit, with very little effort involved. If you would like to know more about using your images in this way, I have included some useful resources for you in Chapter 7 and included suggestions for some YouTubers you might like to follow.

One of the key skills you need if you are interested in creating images for a client, or for your own online business, is to effectively use AI image generators to create images that will catch people's attention. The aim of Chapters 5 and 6 in this book is to teach you the skills to produce the images efficiently. But first let's have a look at the types of images that are available using Midjourney.

DOI: 10.1201/9781003541677-3

Graphic Design Elements

Midjourney will generate images in whatever medium you specify. Although you will see a lot of photographic type AI images online, it can also create many other graphic design elements for use in printed documents, product mock-ups, logos, game assets, web content, and social media.

The editor of a newsletter contacted me wanting a cartoon image of someone opening Pandora's box as an illustration for an article he was writing. Here is the image that I generated for him in Midjourney in less than 5 minutes. It was exactly what he wanted!

FIGURE 3.1
Midjourney illustration of Pandora's box.

In Figure 3.2, I have included other examples of digital material generated using Midjourney to show the diversity in the type of material it is capable of.

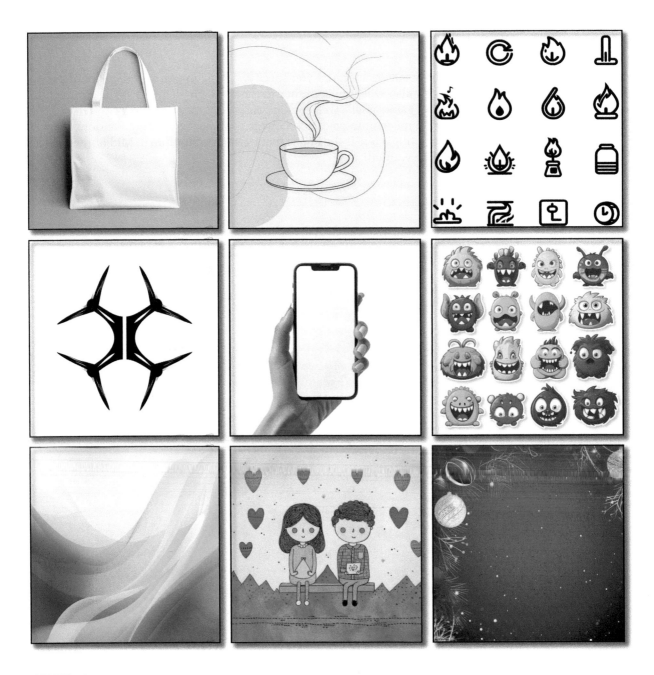

FIGURE 3.2
Examples of digital art materials created in Midjourney.

Images for Cards and Other Products

Midjourney excels at making cute, quirky, attention-grabbing images that look good on cards and other products. One of the great things about Midjourney is you can customize the image to suit a specific occasion, event, or client.

Last Christmas I produced greeting cards for friends, neighbors, and family that were customized to suit their interests or personalities. I have provided two examples in Figure 3.3 that I created – one for a friend who is a potter, and the other who rode a motor bike and owned a greyhound. The images were generated in Midjourney and then imported into Photoshop to add text and turn them into cards.

FIGURE 3.3
Examples of Christmas cards.

Everybody loves receiving something unique and personal – an improvement from the rather boring images on most of the Christmas cards available in the stores. If you are looking for inspiration for images to suit occasions throughout the year Midjourney is a great place to start (see example images in Figure 3.4).

FIGURE 3.4
Example of image for special events.

See Figure 3.5 for examples of other card designs created using Midjourney that I have found sell well.

FIGURE 3.5
Examples of popular card designs.

Backgrounds

Midjourney is great tool for creating backgrounds, patterns, and abstract designs for cards, calendars, products, and advertising (see Figure 3.6). It can replicate a wide variety of different art mediums and you can specify the color, texture, degree of abstraction, and blur that you want.

FIGURE 3.6
Examples of background images.

Book Covers

One of the other creative areas where AI image generation can be applied is the design of book covers. The flexibility and creativity of programs such as Midjourney allows fiction authors to customize the book cover to suit the plot, setting, era, and characters in their novels. It is possible to experiment with alternative designs without the normal cost of producing multiple images using traditional art mediums.

Recently I was contacted by an author who had been struggling to find a cover image for his rather quirky novel. He wanted a Viking ship that had been shipwrecked on a beach on a tropical island in North Queensland, Australia, with palm trees, using a vintage subdued color palette. Not an image you are likely to find in a stock library!

Within a few minutes of experimenting with Midjourney and a few modifications using Adobe Photoshop, I was able to give him what he wanted, and he has used it for his book The Lost Saga (now available on Amazon) (see Figure 3.7).

FIGURE 3.7
Book cover image created using Midjourney.

I have included a few other examples of images that might be suitable for book covers in Figure 3.8.

FIGURE 3.8
Images for book covers.

Wall Art

In playing with Midjourney I have been blown away with the creativity of Midjourney and its ability to produce such a wide variety of "artwork". The examples in Figure 3.9 are the results of my experimenting with images to create as canvases and framed prints.

FIGURE 3.9
Examples of wall art created by Midjourney.

Advertising/Content Creators/Journalists

We live in a world of images. Bombarded from all sides with advertisements, social media, books, magazines, blogs, billboards, and other signage. Until recently these images required an "expert" to produce them – an experienced photographer, graphic artist, or illustrator. The development of programs such as Midjourney has made image creation possible just by typing a few descriptive words on the computer.

This is obviously a much cheaper option for companies wanting content for their websites and advertising material. For example, to create the image of a picnic in the outdoors shown in Figure 3.10 using traditional techniques would have required a photographer, food stylist, hire of a venue, cost of the food and wine, props, and flowers. Instead, I was able to create it by typing a description of the scene (referred to as a prompt) in Midjourney.

FIGURE 3.10
Midjourney image of outdoor picnic.

The added advantage of using AI is that with just a few modifications to the prompt, an alternative image at the beach can be produced with no additional costly fees for a photographer, food stylist, or props (see Figure 3.11).

FIGURE 3.11
Midjourney image of alternative picnic at the beach.

The prompt used to generate images can be adapted to suit the season, location, or mood of the image. This makes it a great tool for advertising, travel magazines, and content creators. Just by changing a few words in the prompt it is possible to get a range of subjects with different characteristics, shot from a variety of different angles, adapted to suit the advertising context (see Figure 3.12).

FIGURE 3.12
Images obtained using different descriptive words in the prompt.

Photographers

Over the past 2 years the quality of the images produced by Midjourney, and other AI image generators, has improved dramatically. This is particularly evident in the photo-realistic images that we are now seeing produced. This has and will continue to have, a serious impact on the work of photographers working in some genres of photography.

AI is a double-edged sword for photographers. On the positive side, AI has been integrated into many of the software packages available, helping to speed up our editing workflow and improve the quality of our images. In 2023 Adobe Lightroom released some amazing improvements in its AI-assisted Masking tools.

From within the Photoshop program, we can now seamlessly remove unwanted elements, extend images, and create totally new material using the Generative Fill tool driven by Adobe's image generator Firefly.

On the potentially negative side, the fact that anyone can generate good-quality images reduces the work available to traditional photographers. This has already impacted on many commercial photographers, particularly those working in advertising, food, and product photography.

According to a recent article in PetaPixel "photographers may have to embrace AI, whether they want to or not".

> While many resist AI, photographers who are adding AI image creation to their armoury may find themselves in a very privileged position—having the ability to offer clients a mix of photos and synthetic photo-style art could prove lucrative.
>
> *Growcoot, 2023*

In the next section, I demonstrate some of the ways that AI images can be used by photographers working in the areas of food, product, advertising, fashion, and portrait photography. This can help to save you time, improve your workflow, and produce more creative images.

Mood Boards and Shot Lists

When planning a photo shoot, it is helpful to prepare a mood board with examples of the types of images that you want to create. This can be provided to the client to clarify their intentions and preferences, and to guide the preparation of the shot list. Instead of using existing images copied from Pinterest, Instagram, and other social media, you can use Midjourney to generate and refine the mood board images. This can often have the unexpected benefit of coming up with ideas you had not thought of!

I have found this particularly helpful when planning fashion and portrait shoots. Prior to the shoot you can explore colors, poses, props, and backgrounds without leaving your studio (see Figure 3.13). It is easy to share these with the model so that they have a good understanding of the look you are after.

FIGURE 3.13
Fashion photography mood board images created in Midjourney.

Midjourney is also a useful tool when planning editorial or documentary-type shoots (stills or videos) that tell a story. I used it last year when planning a documentary series highlighting the problem of loneliness among our elderly citizens.

The series titled "The Age of Loneliness" featured Gloria, my 88-year-old next-door neighbor. To help Gloria understand the images I wanted to capture, I described what I wanted in a prompt for Midjourney, and it obligingly produced a shot list set of images for me. In Figure 3.14, the Midjourney-generated images are shown on the left, and the photographs I took (with a real camera) are on the right.

FIGURE 3.14
Examples of mood board images created in Midjourney and corresponding photographs taken with a camera.
If you would like to see the full series of Age of Loneliness images set to music, go to www.youtube.com/watch?v=H0wU7g5YWCM.

Fashion Photography

One area of photography where AI image generators have proved particularly useful is fashion. Programs like Midjourney can be used to stimulate creativity, experiment with different ideas, and create digital backgrounds and props. It can create mood boards and shot lists for shoot planning and discussion with clients.

In early 2023 the Vogue Italia magazine cover story featured an interesting, and at the time, rather controversial, experiment it described as "when photography plays with Artificial Intelligence". Each of the images in that article represented a collaboration between a model, photographer, stylist, and the DALL-E Artificial Intelligence program.

Images of the model Bella Hadid shot in the studio were superimposed onto artificial backgrounds which were created by the AI image generator DALL-E. Initially, Carlijn Jacobs, the photographer, tried using a series of keywords to get the images he wanted but soon realized "if I wanted to get closer to the idea I had in mind, the precision of my instructions were crucial" (Fossi, 2023). He then hired an AI expert (Chad Nelson) to turn his creative vision into prompts and keywords to feed into DALL-E.

According to the stylist involved in the project:

> the collaboration between Chad and Carlijn was super interesting to watch: Carlijn, with his limitless imagination, stimulated the creativity of AI with ever-changing ideas, which Chad, mastering the art of talking to the machine to perfection, was able to translate into effective prompts.
>
> *Fossi, 2023*

There is a detailed article, featuring an interview with the photographer and stylist, that makes interesting reading: www.vogue.it/article/bella-hadid-cover-vogue-italia-artificial-intelligence-photo. The article is in Italian – you will need to ask your browser to translate for you (unless you happen to speak Italian!).

One of the key points that this article makes is the need for carefully created prompts, describing what you want in your image, presented in such a way that the image generator program can understand. This is one of the key aims of this book – to give you the skills to communicate effectively with Midjourney to obtain the results that you want.

Even if you have a clear idea in your mind, be prepared to capitalize on some of the amazingly creative ideas generated by the program itself. I have been constantly amazed at what is generated – it goes way beyond what I could have imagined myself, introducing quirky combinations, additional unexpected elements, or unusual combinations of art styles (see Figure 3.15).

FIGURE 3.15
Examples of fashion images created by Midjourney.

Midjourney is a good source of ideas for backgrounds, props, and accessories for a fashion shoot (see Figure 3.16).

FIGURE 3.16
Fashion photography props created by Midjourney.

You could also choose to follow the lead of the Vogue Italia magazine and combine images of the model shot in the studio with backgrounds and props generated using Midjourney. For compositing or combining images you will need reasonable skills using Photoshop (or equivalent program that allows you to combine layers). This is discussed in more detail in Chapter 8.

Portrait and Family Photography

Portraits and headshots are one of the genres of photography where AI is not likely to completely take over the job of the photographer anytime soon. There are special times in people's lives when they want their memories captured by someone who knows how to use a "real" camera (as opposed to the millions of happy snaps and selfies taken on an iPhone!).

There are various ways that Midjourney can help those of you that photograph people for a living (or just want more creative images of your family). Instead of purchasing multiple studio backdrops in different colors and patterns, you can ask Midjourney to generate them for you, customizing them to suit your client's needs and preferences.

Photograph your clients against a white or gray background and in Photoshop remove the background and replace it with the Midjourney image. This process is becoming easier in Photoshop with all the AI-assisted tools that help you select a subject, remove backgrounds, swap out skies, delete unwanted elements, or create additional material.

In Midjourney you can make these backgrounds as creative as you like. They can be a single color, textured, or themed (e.g., Christmas). They can feature background images such as curtains, rooms, staircases, gardens, waterfalls, office environments, or any customized setting you want.

I routinely use digital backgrounds I create in Midjourney for my portraits – often color matched to suit the client's outfit. In the example shown in Figure 3.17, I photographed my client Jill on a simple white paper background and then dropped three different Midjourney backgrounds in Photoshop to create three quite different looks. I have a very small studio, so I find this much more convenient than stopping and changing backdrops during the shoot.

FIGURE 3.17
Examples of portrait background replacement. (Author images copyright © Julie Pallant.)

Other examples of backgrounds generated in Midjourney are shown in Figure 3.18.

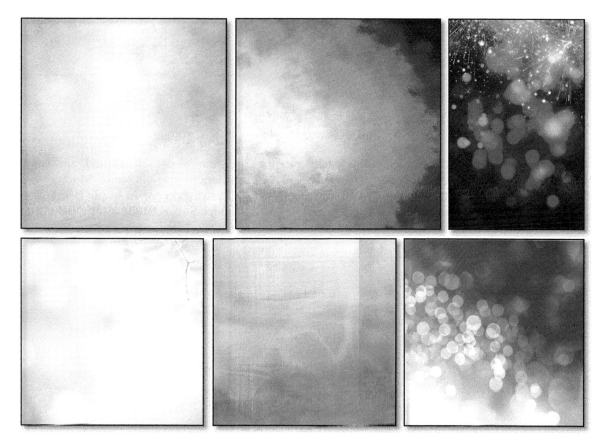

FIGURE 3.18
Examples of background images for portraits created in Midjourney.

The benefit of using Midjourney to create backgrounds for portrait shoots is that you are only limited by your imagination. You can experiment with different colors, textures, themes, and locations to suit the client or occasion (see Figure 3.19).

FIGURE 3.19
Midjourney location images for portraits.

Another great use of Midjourney is to create backdrops for Christmas shoots. It is quick and easy to shoot your client against a white background and to cut and paste them into the scene. Much cheaper than purchasing pre-printed Christmas backdrops – and easier to store! In the example below I shot this family against white, cut them out using the AI-assisted **Select Subject** tool in Photoshop, and pasted them into the Midjourney background I created. I generated six different backgrounds for them to choose from.

FIGURE 3.20
Example of composited image of family using Midjourney Christmas backdrop.

For presenting images to clients, you can generate room mock-ups in Midjourney (see Figure 3.21). In Photoshop you can then insert the images that you have shot of the client. This can help to improve your sales as clients appreciate being able to visualize how their photo will look on the wall.

FIGURE 3.21
Room mockups created using Midjourney.

When shooting families, it is often helpful to prepare a mood board of ideas for images that might be included in the photoshoot. Midjourney can be used to generate examples to share with your client beforehand and to stimulate ideas during the shoot itself. These can be customized to suit the characteristics of your client by specifying the nationality, the number and age of children, and location (see Figure 3.22).

FIGURE 3.22
Mood board of family portrait images created in Midjourney.

Food Photography

Even at this early stage of its development Midjourney does a pretty good job of producing images of food suitable for use online and in advertising. It is quicker, simpler (and less messy) to produce these AI images than it is to hire a photographer, food stylist, venue, and equipment.

It is not surprising that some clients are choosing to employ staff skilled in AI, rather than the more expensive food photographer. Fortunately for those of us that shoot photos with cameras for a living, there are clearly situations where real, authentic food photos are needed. AI images can still be helpful in these situations – they can serve as inspiration when planning a shoot, or to use in a mood board for discussion with a client (see Figure 3.23).

FIGURE 3.23
Examples of food photography images created using Midjourney.

If props are needed, or additional food that is not available (e.g. fruit that is out of season), you can composite AI images into photographs for creative effect. Having both photographic expertise, and the ability to produce appropriate AI images, is a useful combination of skills to have.

Product Photography

Product photography is another area where the combination of good photography skills and the ability to generate AI images is a winning combination. Midjourney is a useful tool to spark creativity and quickly and easily generate ideas for product photoshoots. Mood boards created using AI images can be shared with clients to discuss proposed images and to clarify what is wanted. Mock-ups, backgrounds, and props can be created simply and cheaply, and modified to suit the situation (see Figure 3.24).

FIGURE 3.24
Examples of product photography images created using Midjourney.

Bird, Animal, and Pet Photography

When creating backdrops, you don't have to limit yourself to just fashion or product photography. I use abstract, painted backgrounds generated in Midjourney to enhance images that I take of birds.

I produce and sell a range of my bird images on canvas where I swap out the background for something a bit artier than the twigs and branches that birds usually hang out in. In the example shown in Figure 3.25 you can see the original photograph of a macaw taken at a zoo, the background generated in Midjourney, and the final image where I have merged the two images in Photoshop. More details on how I create these images are provided in Chapter 8.

FIGURE 3.25
Bird photograph merged with a background image created using Midjourney.

I print the composited images as large canvases, framed prints, cards, and coasters that I sell through local galleries and craft markets. I love the fact that I can show the beauty of birds, in a "painterly" way that people want to hang on their walls. The same approach can be used for pet portraits (see Figure 3.26).

FIGURE 3.26
Pet composite images created by merging a photograph with a Midjourney background image.

Midjourney is a useful tool for exploring ideas for projects, exhibitions, competitions, or fine art pieces. I was interested in ideas for an exhibition that would include the image of a person, superimposed over a photograph taken of them when they were younger. Two of the images that Midjourney created are shown in Figure 3.27.

FIGURE 3.27
Midjourney images generated as ideas for an exhibition.

Traditional Artists

Artists are likely to be one of the groups most dramatically affected by the development of artificial intel ligence. An image that may take an experienced, traditional artist many days to create, can instead be rendered in a few moments by someone with no art training using Midjourney. This is certainly an area of considerable concern and controversy, but there are also opportunities to be explored if you are prepared to keep an open mind.

Rather than viewing AI as a rival, artists might like to consider it a tool for expanding their creative horizons. By integrating AI into their practice, artists can explore new areas of creativity, pushing the boundaries of their work in unexpected ways. The key for traditional artists lies in leveraging AI to enhance their own unique vision and skills, ensuring that the soul and emotion that only human experience can impart to art is retained.

I have taught Midjourney to a number of artists who now use the tool to explore ideas for new creations and experiment with alternative compositions and combinations of techniques. They then use these AI-generated images as reference images to create artworks using their preferred medium. This is a great way to turbo charge the creative process and get out of a rut!

At a market stall where I was selling my AI artwork, I was chatting with a watercolor artist about the types of images that could be created using AI. She was struggling with a commission to produce illustrations for a children's book. The book was designed to ease the stress of children having to go to hospital for an operation and she wanted an image of a girl in a hospital bed surrounded by birds and flowers. The image shown in Figure 3.28 is one of the images I created in Midjourney for her.

FIGURE 3.28
Midjourney creation as a reference image for watercolor artist.

The Midjourney computers have obviously been trained on a lot of children's books as they do a pretty good job at generating illustrations. I have included a few examples that I created using Midjourney in Figure 3.29. At this stage of Midjourney's development you don't have a lot of control over the content of the images, particularly in terms of maintaining consistent characters across multiple images, however this is likely to improve.

FIGURE 3.29
Examples of children's book illustrations created in Midjourney.

AI image generation is also being used very effectively in the production of artwork for affirmation, oracle, and tarot cards. In Chapter 7, I have included examples of the work of Ayesha Hilton, a digital artist who specializes in this type of art.

Midjourney prompts, which include the words spiritual, mystical, and meditation, produce a range of images that can act as inspiration for the creation of traditional illustrations for spiritually oriented products (see Figure 3.30). This is an area where it is helpful to have a combination of good Midjourney prompt skills with traditional and digital art skills to customize a unique design.

FIGURE 3.30
Examples of spiritually themed images created in Midjourney.

Midjourney has been trained on a wide variety of art styles and you can ask for an image to be created "in the style of XXX" where you specify an art style or movement or an artist. In addition to specifying the style you want in the written prompt, you can also upload an image that you like the style of as an example for Midjourney.

This allows you to experiment with applying styles to different objects or themes or combining styles to create something completely unique. In the examples shown in Figure 3.31, I asked Midjourney for images of a mother and child, specifying different art styles for each.

FIGURE 3.31
Examples of Midjourney creations showing different art styles.

Teachers and Parents

As AI image generation becomes more sophisticated and integrated into educational systems, there will be a shift toward providing more personalized, efficient, and engaging learning opportunities for our children. The ability to instantly generate learning materials that are adapted to suit the particular needs and interests of the child makes it a very powerful tool for teachers and parents alike.

Not only can AI image generators be used by educators to produce teaching materials, but they can also provide children with the opportunity to participate in the creative process themselves. Programs such as Midjourney can be used by parents with their children in a variety of ways to help entertain, educate, and stimulate creativity. I have listed below a few ways that you might like to use AI-generated art with your children, adapted to suit their age and interests.

Artistic Expression

Encourage your child to explore their creativity with AI art tools. These tools can help them generate unique artwork, experiment with different styles, and stimulate their creativity. These artworks could also be used as a reference image for the child to reproduce the image using more traditional art mediums, such as water colors and acrylic paint. This can give them a greater appreciation for the skills of traditional artists.

Educational Projects

Programs such as Midjourney are a valuable tool for students when creating images as part of school projects. These images help the child visualize historical scenes or events, literary characters or settings, scientific concepts (e.g., solar system, see Figure 3.32), or to create materials relating to special occasions or events (e.g., Thanksgiving, Mother's Day).

FIGURE 3.32
Image of Saturn created by Midjourney.

Storytelling

Sharing AI-generated images with your child can also help to inspire creative writing or storytelling. Your child can describe the scene, characters, or events depicted in the image. Alternatively, the child can make up a story, and then use an AI-image generator to produce illustrations, helping to bring their story to life (see Figure 3.33).

FIGURE 3.33
Example of creating Midjourney images from a child's story.

Personalized Learning and Play Materials

Midjourney can be used to create customized images and illustrations for your child's coloring books, flashcards, alphabet, and counting books. These can be tailored to suit the child's specific interests (e.g., dinosaurs, unicorns, and spaceships).

I have a 4-year-old granddaughter who absolutely loves unicorns so I have produced coloring books featuring a little girl (who actually looks very much like her) playing with a unicorn (see Figure 3.34).

FIGURE 3.34
Children's coloring book page created in Midjourney.

If the books you create prove popular, you might consider uploading them for sale to print-on-demand sites such as Amazon. I have provided ideas for more money-making opportunities in Chapter 8.

Family Fun

If you are looking for creative activities that the family can engage in together you might like to consider:

- creating materials for interactive card games (e.g., Snap, Memory) using images that have meaning for family members
- creating personalized greeting cards
- generating funny images or memes
- designing imaginary worlds or characters for storytelling

A great family activity is creating gifts using AI images uploaded to print-on-demand websites (e.g., Redbubble.com). Images can be used to create jigsaw puzzles, placemats, stickers, water bottles, clothing, pillows, and bed linen. What a buzz for a child to wear a T-shirt featuring an image that he/she created! I have provided more information on print-on-demand in Chapter 8.

In this increasingly commercialized world, it is very satisfying to create a gift that is meaningful to the person and not a mass-produced item from a shop. I created the image shown in Figure 3.35 to use on a birthday card for my 5-year-old grandson who is obsessed with karate. He was so excited to receive it and loved the fact that the character looked like him. The ability to customize the image to suit the child and their interests is one of the real strengths of programs like Midjourney.

FIGURE 3.35
Midjourney image for my grandson's birthday card.

Teaching Materials in Schools

AI image generators can be utilized by teachers in primary and secondary schools to create images to be incorporated into various subjects across the curriculum, including:

- History (bringing historical scenes and events to life)
- Science (scientific illustrations, diagrams, and illustration of scientific processes)
- English Language Arts (creative writing, storytelling, creation of comics/graphic novels, and multimedia presentations)
- Art (digital art and mixed media)
- Emotional Intelligence (generate images depicting different emotions, e.g., happy, sad, and angry), and ask children to identify and describe the emotions.

AI generated images are a very powerful tool for students to use in projects raising awareness of social and environmental issues. Images generated by Midjourney have the advantage of being copyright-free, so they can be used publicly to promote events such as World Environment Day (5th June), World Ocean Day (8th June), and World Soil Day (5th December) (see examples in Figure 3.36).

FIGURE 3.36
Images to promote awareness of environmental issues.

Developing Children's Knowledge and Skills in AI Image Generation

As students prepare to leave school and enter the workforce, having proficiency in AI image generation will be a highly valuable skill set to possess. In today's rapidly evolving job market, industries such as business, marketing, graphic design, and communications are increasingly relying on AI-powered tools to create engaging visual content.

Students who have these skills will have a competitive edge in the job market, setting them apart from others and opening up more career opportunities. As AI technology continues to advance, the demand for professionals who can work effectively with AI image generators will only continue to grow, making it an essential skill for futureproofing your child's career.

Across all areas of curriculum, teachers should encourage students to embrace the new AI software and to use it to create visual components for projects, presentations, and posters. If you are a teacher, or a parent of a child in secondary school, I encourage you to develop your own skills and expertise in image generation to provide support, encouragement, and enhance opportunities for your student's learning.

Therapists

Art and creative activities have long been recognized as powerful therapeutic tools, offering significant mental health benefits. Engaging in artistic expression is a good way to explore emotions, manage stress, and enhance mindfulness in a non-verbal way. This form of therapy, often referred to as art therapy, typically involves activities like drawing, painting, sculpture, and collage, that enable individuals to express thoughts and feelings that they find difficult to articulate through conventional language. Art therapy has been shown to improve self-esteem and confidence by allowing individuals to accomplish creative tasks and see tangible results of their efforts.

AI image generators are a potentially useful tool for therapists as they offer a new medium for creative expression and emotional exploration. They are quick and easy to learn and they do not require an artistic background or previous training.

Listed below are some ways AI image generators can be used in art therapy:

Accessibility

AI image generators can be especially helpful for individuals who struggle with traditional art-making due to physical or cognitive limitations. With AI image generators, anyone can create art, regardless of their age, skill level, or abilities. They do not require expensive equipment or tools, and they can be used any time of the day or night, in any environment.

Emotional Expression

AI image generators can be used to create visual representations of emotions, thoughts, and experiences. This can be particularly helpful for individuals who struggle with verbal communication, or find it difficult to express themselves through traditional art forms. They can use their AI images to portray what they feel inside, opening the communication channels with their family, friends, and therapists.

I have included a few examples in Figure 3.37 of Midjourney images representing a variety of emotional experiences.

FIGURE 3.37
Midjourney images representing a range of emotions.

Stress Reduction and Relaxation

In a recent study, researchers found that viewing soothing images of nature had positive effects on participants' mood and well-being and significantly decreased anxiety and depression levels (Witten et al., 2022). They suggest that this could be incorporated into therapeutic practices in the treatment of a range of mental health conditions (Witten et al., 2022). The images used in this study were obtained from Project Soothe (www.projectsoothe.com) which collects soothing images from the public, the most popular being landscapes, water features, trees, flowers, and animals.

Generating and looking at AI images that are calming, uplifting, or inspiring is an easy way for someone who experiences anxiety or depression to modify their emotions (see examples in Figure 3.38). Images can be custom designed to suit the individual and their personal preferences. They can be used as screen savers for computers or TV screens, printed and displayed on the wall, or incorporated into a book.

FIGURE 3.38
Calming images generated using Midjourney.

Researchers at the University of Leeds have found that viewing images of cute animals can reduce stress levels by 50% (School of Biomedical Sciences News, 2020). If there is one thing that Midjourney does well, it is to make cute images of kittens and puppies! (see Figure 3.39).

FIGURE 3.39
Cute images generated using Midjourney.

Collaboration and Communication

AI image generators can facilitate collaboration between therapists, clients, family members, and the wider community. Creating art together and sharing images can foster deeper connections and understanding – promoting a sense of community and shared experience.

There are many Facebook sites that allow people to share their AI images with other creatives across the globe. For many, this provides a welcome opportunity to connect with like-minded people and to grow friendships and support groups. In Chapter 7, I report on an interview I did with one of the women who administers a Facebook group that has over 28,000 members that provides a safe place for people to share their AI creations.

Personal Growth and Empowerment

The process of producing images can help individuals develop a sense of pride, confidence, and self-worth. Seeing their ideas brought to life can be incredibly empowering, promoting personal growth and self-awareness.

By incorporating AI image generators into art therapy, therapists, and clients can explore new avenues for creative expression, emotional exploration, and personal growth. I have seen this myself with people that I have taught Midjourney – there is an excitement and sense of wonder at the art they have been able to create. This is a powerful mood-boosting tool for those in the community struggling with stress, anxiety, and depression, or anyone that just needs cheering up!

References

Fossi, M. (2023, 27 April). Bella Hadid on the cover of Vogue Italia: When photography plays with artificial intelligence. *Vogue Italia*. www.vogue.it/article/bella-hadid-cover-vogue-italia-artificial-intelligence-photo

Growcoot, M. (2023, December 28). The AI images that shook the photography world in 2023. *Petapixel*. https://petapixel.com/2023/12/28/the-ai-images-that-shook-the-photography-world-in-2023

School of Biomedical Sciences News. (2020, 7 October). What are the health benefits of watching cute animals. *Faculty of Biological Sciences, University of Leeds*. https://biologicalsciences.leeds.ac.uk/school-biomedical-sciences/news/article/273/what-are-the-health-benefits-of-watching-cute-animals

Witten, E., Ryynanen, J., Wisdom, S., Tipp, C., and Chan, S. (2022). Effects of soothing images and soothing sounds on mood and well-being. *British Journal of Clinical Psychology, 62*(1), 158–179.

4

AI Image-Generating Programs

Introduction

With the rapid evolution of AI technology over the last 2 years there has been an explosion of AI image generation programs that have come onto the scene. Some are stand alone, and others have been integrated into platforms, search engines and photo editing programs such as Adobe Photoshop. Some programs are free, while others require a subscription to use. The list is growing every day with new developments and advances in the field.

Choosing the right tool for your creative project can be a daunting task, as each program has its own unique strengths, weaknesses, and characteristics. From popular options like Midjourney, DALL-E, and Stable Diffusion, to newer programs that have appeared recently such as Meta AI, the options seem endless. In choosing the program you need to weigh up factors like image quality, style versatility, ease of use, and cost. Knowing which program to use is difficult when you are only starting out with image generation – the jargon and terminology is confusing and all of the program developers claim that their program is the best.

In this chapter, I provide you with a list of some of the major players in the image generation field, and I explain why I have chosen to use and recommend Midjourney.

List of AI Programs

In the following table, I have included a list of some of the most well-known of AI image generators, but depending on when you are reading this book there may be many others that have come onto the scene.

Name	Description	Website
Midjourney	Very powerful and flexible program. Web-based interface. Requires a paid subscription – but well worth the cost.	https://www.midjourney.com/
DALL-E 3	DALL-E-3 is available through OpenAI platform and is incorporated into CHATGPT.	https://openai.com/dall-e-3
Firefly (Adobe)	Free version available. The premium version requires a subscription to ADOBE. Available as a standalone and also integrated into other ADOBE programs – Photoshop, Adobe Express, and Illustrator.	https://firefly.adobe.com/
Stable Diffusion	There are a number of different versions of Stable Diffusion. It is available online, or if you have good tech skills it can be installed onto your own computer. Free and paid versions are available. Images generated on the free version have a watermark.	https://stablediffusionweb.com/

DOI: 10.1201/9781003541677-4

Name	Description	Website
Image Creator (Microsoft)	This is powered by a more advanced version of DALL-E. It is free to use but requires a Microsoft account. It is also available through Windows Copilot.	https://copilot.microsoft.com/
Meta AI	Free to use program that provides both text-generation and image-generation.	https://ai.meta.com/
Leonardo AI	Free and paid version of the program.	https://leonardo.ai/

This list will become out of date almost the moment it is written, given the rapid advances in the field and the influx of new programs and apps. Programs also have a habit of changing names or being incorporated into different platforms.

While some of these AI programs offer free versions, you need to be aware that they may have limitations on the number of free generations they allow. Some free programs also apply a watermark to their images. The quality of the generated image, ease of use, and additional features, such as the ability to work via both text and image prompts, are important factors to consider when choosing an AI image generator.

What each of the image-generating programs have in common is the ability to generate an image by inputting a text "prompt". Basically, this is a description of what you want included in the image. This can be as simple as asking for a cute kitten or as complex as describing a scene with multiple elements set in a specific time period, using the style of an art movement or era.

When you are first starting out you might like to experiment with one or more of the free programs listed above. You may be able to meet your image generation needs with a free program, but generally I have found the quality and sophistication of the images is much higher using the paid programs. This is particularly important if you are a professional intending to use an AI image generator to produce images for clients or for sale.

Midjourney

Overview

After exploring the various image generator programs available, I chose to use Midjourney due to its versatility, user-friendly interface, and the quality of the images it produces. Midjourney's ability to generate images with remarkable detail and realism makes it the ideal choice for my specific creative needs. Midjourney's community-based approach, where you can see other people's artwork and prompts, has made the learning process so much easier.

While other programs like DALL-E and Stable Diffusion offer unique strengths, Midjourney's overall package of features, ease of use, and consistently high-quality results, I believe makes it the best program currently available. The quality of the images Midjourney produces puts it at the top of the list of programs that I recommend for professionals who need to use image generation as part of their work. According to Donelli (2024) "Midjourney is unparalleled in terms of quality of results and continues to set the bar high".

Midjourney is only available on a monthly subscription plan, which I know is a pain, but it does get regularly updated with more features being added. In my opinion (and many millions of other users), it is well worth the cost given the quality of the images and the flexibility of the prompts that can be used to customize your desired images.

So, what is Midjourney? It is an artificial intelligence program designed to generate images from text descriptions (known as prompts). It allows you to create a wide variety of images, from simple logos through to detailed art works, across a wide range of art styles and genres. It utilizes advanced machine learning algorithms to interpret text inputs and translate them into images that can be used by artists, designers, content creators, and anyone interested in image creation.

I have listed some of Midjourney's key features and capabilities below:

- easy to use web-based interface
- generate high quality images from both text and image prompts
- create artwork in a wide variety of styles, from line drawings through to photo-realistic
- ability to generate images which incorporate text
- upload existing images to use as style and character references
- manipulate and revise existing images
- experiment with different prompts, styles, and variations
- ability to run multiple generations from a single prompt to explore variations
- tools to help categorize and organize images
- search tools to help you find specific images in your online database
- online gallery of user's images and prompts for inspiration
- regular updates and communication from the program developers
- opportunity to have input into the further development of the program

Midjourney was first made available to the public in 2022 and it has been constantly developed and revised since then, with new versions being released every few months. At the time of writing this book (June, 2024) Version 6.0 is the main version in use, although it is likely to have been updated by the time you are reading this book.

With each new update the quality of the images has improved dramatically, and extra features have been added. In the most recent Version 6 the ability to generate text was added and the options for using images as references was improved.

Different Ways to Access Midjourney

Up until early 2024, Midjourney could only be accessed through the Discord platform, which is a digital communication platform commonly used by video gamers and other groups. When you are first starting out this can be rather confusing to get set up.

In February 2024, Midjourney released an online version of the program, but at that time it was only accessible for regular users of Midjourney who had generated 1000 or more images. This was to allow the online platform to be tested and refined based on feedback from regular users. The online version of Midjourney was released to the public on 22 August 2024.

In this book, I provide instructions on how to access Midjourney through the online platform, although the Discord version will continue to be available into the future. If you are watching YouTube videos on Midjourney made before May 2024 it is likely they will be using the Discord version – the same tools are available on the online platform but are easier to use.

A word of warning – Midjourney is constantly refining and improving the program. This means that what you see on your screen may not exactly match the instructions shown in this book.

> If you notice that any of your screens look different to what is shown in the book you can keep up to date with changes to the Midjourney program on my website. You will also find videos showing how you can make the most out of Midjourney.
>
> You can access the website using the link: https://linktr.ee/juliepallant

Getting the Best Out of Midjourney

Producing an AI-generated image is a creative partnership between humans and machines. It's a collaborative process where the person providing the prompt brings their ideas, imagination, and direction, while the computer contributes its processing power, algorithms, and generative capabilities.

You might like to think of it as a conversation: you provide the initial idea or prompt, and the program responds with an image. You can then refine your prompt, and the AI adjusts its output. This back-and-forth process allows you to guide the AI's creativity, shaping the final image.

In this collaboration, the human provides the creative vision, while the AI executes it. The AI doesn't simply create the image on its own; it's a tool that interprets human imagination via the prompt that it is provided. By working together, humans and AI can produce unique and stunning images.

The quality and suitability of the images that you obtain from Midjourney will depend in a large part on the prompt that you write and the way that you describe what you want. Crafting clear, specific, and well-defined prompts is crucial. The quality of the input prompt directly affects the output image. In Chapter 6, I provide a detailed guide, with examples, on how to write good prompts. As an introduction, I have summarized a few of the key points below:

- **Be specific**: Provide clear and detailed prompts to help the AI understand what you want.
- **Use relevant keywords**: Include relevant keywords and phrases to guide the AI's generation process.
- **Define the style**: Specify the desired style, tone, and mood to get an image that fits your vision.
- **Reference images**: Provide reference images or examples to help the AI understand your visual preferences.
- **Experiment with prompts**: Try different prompts and variations to find what works best.
- **Use appropriate parameters**: Adjust resolution, aspect ratio, and file format to suit your needs.
- **Refine and iterate**: Refine your prompts based on the AI's output and iterate until you get the desired result.
- **Understand the model's limitations**: Know what the AI can and cannot do to set realistic expectations.
- **Post-processing**: Be prepared to edit the generated image to enhance or refine it further.

Take an experimental approach to using Midjourney – this means being prepared to rerun prompts as it is unlikely that you will get exactly what you want first time around. Try adding, subtracting, and replacing words in your prompt, and rearranging the order they are listed. You may find this frustrating at first, but it is just part of the experience when using new emerging technology – it makes it even more exciting when you do get the image that you wanted (or something even better!).

One thing to keep in mind when using Midjourney (and indeed any AI image generator) is that each of the images that are created are unique. When you type in a prompt the program is not searching its database for an existing image that matches your request. Instead, it is creating the image from scratch, drawing on information it has been taught from the enormous databases of images that it was trained on. This means that each time you use a specific prompt you will get a different image. Keep this in mind when you are reading this book – if you experiment by running the prompts that I provide, you will not get the same image as I did.

If you are requesting an image of something that the computer has not been trained on, for example some very rare animal, remote location, or a new invention it has not been exposed to, it may not be able to produce your requested image. You can try uploading an image of your own of the object that you want included and ask Midjourney to include this in the image – this can be very hit and miss.

Like any image generator program, the output from Midjourney can be very unpredictable and sometimes downright weird. It may produce images with distorted faces, hands with a few fingers, and add unusual limbs. These weird images were very common in the earlier versions of Midjourney but can still sometimes appear when using a recent version.

Midjourney has shown some dramatic improvements over the past 2 years and will continue to improve into the future. To illustrate this improvement in Figure 4.1, I have included one of the less successful generations I obtained when using a much earlier version of Midjourney (Version 4). I then repeated the same **prompt:** fairy, flying, pink, full length, photograph, fantasy, gold foil, Gustav Klimt style using the latest version (Version 6) (see the results in Figure 4.2).

FIGURE 4.1
Image created in Midjourney Version 4 showing distorted face and hands, three arms.

FIGURE 4.2
Image created in Midjourney Version 6 showing much improved features.

One final piece of advice before we get stuck into learning Midjourney – don't expect too much from the program. Despite the advances that have occurred over the past few years, Midjourney has its limitations and it will rarely give you exactly the image that you want. To achieve your objective, it may be necessary to edit your AI-generated image to remove unwanted elements, adjust color and tone, or add text.

Additional programs such as Adobe Photoshop are very useful to have in your toolkit for this purpose. Photoshop gives you the control to make precise modifications to your image, which is not yet possible in Midjourney. In recent years, many AI-assisted tools have been incorporated in Photoshop making the editing of images so much easier. In Chapter 8, I provide examples of how I use Photoshop to enhance, modify, and composite the output from Midjourney to create the images that I need.

Reference

Donelli, F. (2024, January 13). Generative AI in fashion imagery: A current assessment and future outlook. *Medium*. https://medium.com/@fdonelli/generative-ai-in-fashion-imagery-a-current-assessment-and-future-outlook-45ef059e911f

5

Getting Started with Midjourney

Introduction

In this book I will get you started with Midjourney using the online platform. Prior to March 2024 we needed to access Midjourney through Discord, a gaming platform which many people found confusing to set up. Now that Midjourney is accessible directly through their website things are a lot easier!

It is quick and easy to generate images with Midjourney – it just involves typing a description of what you want in the box at the top of the screen. However, you may not always get the image that you want – this is where the art of "promptology" comes in. This involves learning how to communicate with Midjourney to get the best possible results.

In this chapter, I will take you on a tour of the Midjourney website and explain how to use the basics of the program. This will get you started producing images, without overwhelming you with too much information. In Chapter 6, I will take you deeper into the features available in Midjourney to fine tune your prompts.

Before we start there are a couple of points you need to understand about Midjourney. Every image that you create in Midjourney will be unique. Even if you use the exact prompt that I use in the examples in the book you will not get the same image – in fact sometimes it will be dramatically different! Even if you repeat the same prompt twice you will get different results. This is particularly the case if you use a very short prompt that does not provide Midjourney with much information.

It is rare that you will get exactly the image that you want with your first attempt. Be prepared to rerun images, change the words that you use, and the order that they are presented. Experiment with adding in words, removing them, and applying different parameters (these will be explained later). I see people start using Midjourney, run a few prompts, and then give up because they don't like the images. It can take me up to ten attempts to get an image that I am happy with!

The images that you create in Midjourney can be seen by other users, unless you pay for the Pro-Plan which offers a **Stealth** mode that hides your images from the public forums. Midjourney works on a community-based model where users can learn from each other by seeing the images others produce and what prompts were used to create them.

Being able to see other people's images is an advantage when you are first starting out and trying to learn about prompt writing. The disadvantage is that other Midjourney users can copy your prompts to create their own images – in fact they can download and save images that you created. There is no copyright on images generated in Midjourney.

DOI: 10.1201/9781003541677-5

Set Up a Midjourney Account

Midjourney is a subscription-based program so you will need to set up an account with Midjourney and provide your credit card details. Go to the Midjourney website (www.midjourney.com) and sign up for an account.

There are a number of subscription plans to choose from and you can elect to pay monthly or yearly. If you are just starting out, I suggest you choose monthly billing which allows you to pay as you go along. Note that the prices quoted on the website are in US dollars as at March 2024.

For your first month I recommend you start with the **Standard Plan** which allows unlimited generations. The cheaper **Basic Plan** only allows 200 images per month which you could use up in a few days when you start playing with the program! On a monthly payment plan you can easily change plans, or cancel at any time, if you decide Midjourney is not for you.

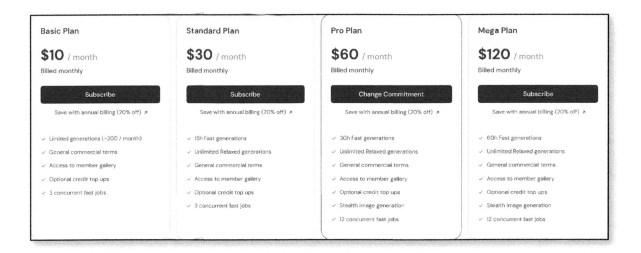

The Midjourney Workspace

Let's start with a quick tour of the workspace that you will see when you open the program. Your screen may look different to those shown in the examples below. At the time of writing this manual (June 2024), the online version of Midjourney was still in the alpha phase being tested before its general release to the public. Midjourney is constantly updating its software and adding new features and rearranging buttons – so be prepared to adapt.

If you notice that any of your screens look different to what is shown in the book you can keep up to date with changes to the Midjourney program on my website. You will also find videos showing how you can make the most out of Midjourney.

You can access the website using the link: https://linktr.ee/juliepallant

On the left-hand side of the Midjourney screen you will see a number of options:

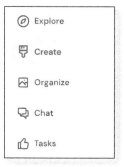

Explore – view images created by other users of Midjourney

Create – the area where you create your own images

Organize – record of all the images you have created

Chat – option to interact with other users

Tasks – use this button to access:

   Rate Images – to provide feedback on images to help improve the program

   Rate Ideas – submit ideas you have for improving the program

At the bottom of the screen is another set of buttons:

Help – access to **Documentation, Billing Support,** and **Report a Bug** for reporting issues with the program.

Updates – information about changes to the program.

Light Mode/ Dark Mode – allows you to toggle between a white screen (Light Mode) or a black screen (Dark Mode). I used Light Mode for the screen shots in this book.

Click on the button showing your user-name to access **Manage Subscription**, **Manage Uploads** and **Log Out**.

Create an Image

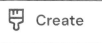

To begin the creation process, click on the **Create** button (it may show as a paintbrush) on the left-hand side of the screen.

Type a description of the image that you want to create in the **prompt** box.

Later in this book I will be explaining how to write a good image description (referred to as a **prompt**). When you are first starting out, feel free to just have a play and describe whatever you like.

   The prompt I used in this example is shown as follows.

Prompt: photograph in a café, a glass of orange juice, plate of bacon and eggs on toast, a steaming cup of coffee on a wooden table

You might like to follow along on your computer – remember that you will not get exactly the same image as shown here. Each time you generate an image it will be unique.

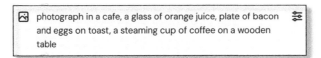

Press **Enter** on your keyboard to activate the command. This can take a few minutes, particularly during busy times!
    Midjourney will give you a grid with four images to choose from.

Click on one of the images and it will open full screen.

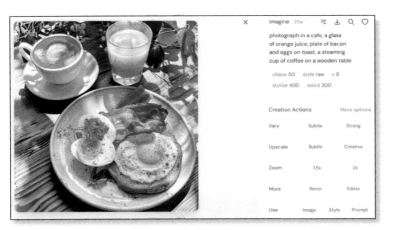

In the top right of the screen you will see the prompt that was used to generate the image.

On the bottom right is a set of commands that you can use to modify the image.

When you want to return to the main window to see the other images, click on the **Create** button. First though, I will take you on a tour of the commands on the bottom right of the screen that you can use to modify the image that you have chosen. This menu will only appear when you have selected a single image in the **Create** section.

Upscale and Save an Image

If you find an image that you want to save, first you need to **Upscale** it. This is an important step as the initial images generated by Midjourney are small, low-resolution images. Upscaling enlarges the image and gives it more detail.

You can choose between **Upscale (Subtle)** which keeps the image close to the original, or **Upscale (Creative)** which varies the image creatively (I tend to use **Subtle**). You might like to experiment to see what results you get with each option.

Click on the **Upscale** button of your choice and Midjourney will process the image.

Repeat this process with any of the four images that you wish to upscale.

To review the upscaled image/s click **Create**, and then on the image thumb-nail to make it full screen.

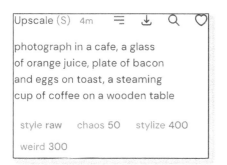

To save the upscaled image to your computer click on the download icon (down pointing arrow) on the right-hand side of the screen.

Midjourney will save the image to the Downloads file on your computer.

The file name consists of your user-name, followed by part of the prompt you used, and an ID number.

Make Variations to an Image

Midjourney gives you the opportunity to explore variations of the images that you create. To view an image, click on it to enlarge it on the screen and you will see a set of buttons appear on the bottom right of the image.

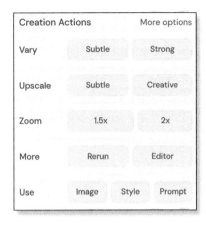

Vary:

Vary (Subtle) or **Vary (Strong)** buttons are used to generate a set of four new images that vary aspects of the image, while keeping to the same basic idea.

Upscale: These buttons are used to enlarge and prepare the image for saving and downloading.

Editor:
Options in this section allow you to:
• change the aspect ratio.
• extend your image up, down, left and right.
• zoom your image out by 1.1x, 1.5x 2x.
• make changes to specific areas of the image and rerun the prompt.
• make changes to the prompt and rerun.

Use:
The **Image** button will include the image in a new prompt.
Style will use the image in the prompt and apply the style to a new image.
Prompt copies the existing prompt up into the **prompt** box for you to run again with modifications.

In the next sections I demonstrate how to use these variations and show the effect they have on my cafe breakfast image.

Vary

When I clicked the **Vary (Subtle) button** Midjourney changed the number of eggs, the type of glass for the orange juice, and added a spoon to one of the coffee cups (see the four images it generated below).

Zoom

If you would like to zoom out and include more of the background, click on the **Zoom** buttons which are located in the **Creation Actions** section on the bottom right of the screen.

You can choose the **1.5x** or **2x Zoom** buttons.

In this example I pressed the **Zoom 1.5x** button to make a bit more room around the edge of the image.

You can see in Figure 5.1 that extra material has been added to all sides, matching the content of the existing image. Pretty clever!

FIGURE 5.1
Output from Zoom.

For more flexibility with expanding your image, you might like to use the **Editor** button (described in the next section).

Editor

With a single image from the grid selected and enlarged, click on the **Editor** button on the bottom right-hand side of the screen to access an integrated set of tools that you can use to change your image. Please note the **Editor** feature is not available for any images that you have upscaled.

A new window will open, providing options to change your aspect ratio, zoom out, extend the image, and to edit specific parts of the image.

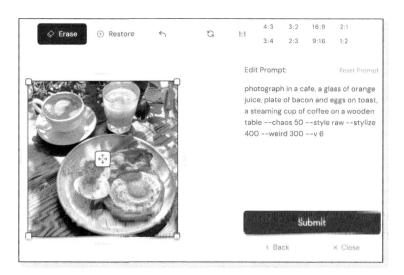

To change the **aspect ratio** of the image, click on one of the options listed in the top right of the **Editor** window.

The aspect ratio buttons in the top row will give you a wide, short image (landscape orientation), while the buttons on the bottom row will give you tall, thinner images (portrait orientation).

Click on the **Submit** button to run the command.

In this example I chose the **2:3** aspect ratio button. Midjourney added extra material to the top and bottom of my image (see Figure 5.2).

FIGURE 5.2
The image after changing the aspect ratio to 2:3.

If you would like to have more control over the expansion of your image you can use the **Scale** slider.

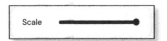

Drag your **Scale** slider to the left to zoom your image out to include more background.

As you drag the **Scale** slider you will see a checkboard pattern showing the extra areas that Midjourney will fill in.

You are not limited to expanding your image equally on all sides.

Click on the 4 arrows icon in the center of the image and hold it down as you drag the image around within the frame.

This allows you to position the image wherever you like, adding more space to the top, bottom, or sides.

In this example I have moved my image to the bottom right of the screen. Midjourney will fill in the checkerboard areas at the left and top.

For even more control over the shape and composition of your image you can click and drag on one of the four gray bars outside of the checkerboard area to adjust the aspect ratio of the image.

While you are in the **Editor** window you can also make modifications to the contents of your image. In this example I wanted to change the glass of "orange juice" to "tomato juice".

The first step is to show Midjourney where in the image the change should occur.

Click on the **Erase** button and paint over the area of the image that you want to change.

In this example I painted over the glass of orange juice. This area was replaced with a checkerboard pattern.

If necessary, you can adjust the size of the brush using the slider with a small dot on the left and a large one on the right.

The next step is to modify the prompt, telling Midjourney what you want in the image.

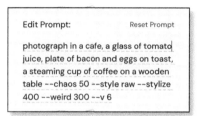

In this example I deleted the words "orange juice" on the top line of the prompt and replaced them with "tomato juice".

Press the **Submit** button to run the modified prompt.

Figure 5.3 shows one of the images that I obtained using **Edit prompt** where I asked for tomato juice, instead of orange juice.

FIGURE 5.3
Output obtained by editing the prompt.

Use

In the **Use** section at the bottom of the **Creation Actions** section are three buttons.

The three options in the **Use** section (**Image, Style, Prompt**) give you the opportunity to use aspects of the selected image in a new prompt.

Image: If you click on this button the image will be added to the prompt box to act as a guide to Midjourney for the content, color, and style of the image that you want to create next.

Style: Using this button tells Midjourney to reproduce the overall look of the image, but not necessarily the content.

Prompt: Pressing this button moves the original prompt up into the prompt box. You can then modify the words in the prompt to suit your needs.

You can choose to click on both the **Image** and the **Prompt** buttons to move them up into the prompt box – this will give you a closer match to the original image. The use of images in prompts will be covered in more detail in Chapter 6.

TIP: In this section I have covered various ways that you can make changes to your images and explore more of the possibilities that Midjourney offers. Don't stop at the first set of images that are generated. Keep rerunning and varying the prompts to see what you can get. Some of my best images have come from accidental discoveries as I experimented with the various options in Midjourney.

Other Useful Tools in Create

When you generate an image in the **Create** module and click to enlarge it, you will see four icons on the right-hand side of the screen. One of these is the **Download** tool which I covered in an earlier section. We will now take a look at what the other icons do.

Hide an Image

While experimenting with Midjourney it is inevitable that you will generate images that you don't like. In the current version of Midjourney there is no way to delete images – but it is possible to hide them from display.

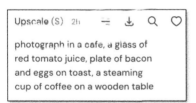

With the image selected in **Create** click on the icon of a set of three horizontal lines.

In the pop out box that appears click on the **Hide image** icon.

This will hide the image from being displayed in your **Archive** of images.

Add a "like" to an Image

On the far right in the set of icons is a heart symbol.

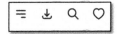

Click on the heart if you like the image you have created.

You will be able to filter your images later and just show the ones that you have "liked".

This is very helpful when you have generated hundreds of images, and you want to find the best ones. I will demonstrate how to use filters later in this chapter.

Search for a Prompt

In the **Create** module on the top right is a **Search prompts** box.

Use this to search through the images you have created for those with a particular word in the prompt.

For example, to find all the cafe images that I generated I would type *cafe* in the **Search prompts** box.

To find the cafe images that featured tomato juice I would type: *cafe, tomato*. Only images with prompts that include both words will be shown.

Press the **X** to turn off the search filter and display all images again.

Organize

The **Organize** menu on the left hand side of the screen is where all the images you have ever created are stored.

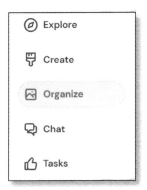

Click on the **Organize** button on the left-hand side of the screen to open it.

A grid of images will appear with a vertical slide bar on the right that you can use to scroll through your images going back in time. As you hover your cursor over the slide bar you will see dates appear showing when the images were created.

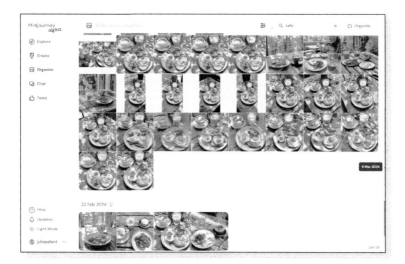

Midjourney provides a number of useful tools to keep your images organized. I have generated over 15,000 images so I certainly make good use of these! In the next few sections I will show you how to set up folders to categorize your images, filters to display images with particular characteristics, and options that allow you to change how you view your images.

Organize Tools

To access the **Folder**, **Filter**, and **View Options** make sure you have the **Organize** module selected on the left hand menu bar.

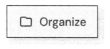

Click on the **Organize** button on the top right corner of the screen.

You should see a box with three sections appear.

The down arrow next to each section indicates they are closed.

When you click on the arrow, each section will open, and the arrow will point upward.

Keep the sections you are not using closed – this makes it easier to navigate around.

View Options

The buttons under **View Options** allow you to change how your images are displayed in the **Archive** section.

Click on the **View Options** arrow to open that section.

In the **Layout** section the **Full** option shows the image at its original aspect ratio, while **Square** displays all thumbnails in a square format.

Image Size allows you to choose how big you want to display your images in the grid.

Small is useful when you want to quickly skim through your images.

Large is helpful when you want a closer look at an image.

Filters

In the **Filters** section you can use a set of tools to filter your archived images so that only images with specific characteristics are shown.

Open the **Filters** section by clicking on the arrow so it is pointing upward

When you open the **Filters** section you will see three subsections.

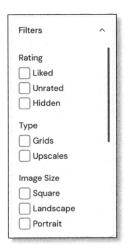

Under **Rating** you can filter to see the images that you liked (that is, clicked on the heart icon). This helps when identifying which images to **Upscale** and to **Download**.

If you want to find an image that you had previously hid you can click on the **Hidden** option to show them here.

Filtering by **Type** and selecting **Upscales** is helpful when you want to identify the images that have been upscaled and are ready to be downloaded.

The **Image Size** filter is useful when you want to find images with a particular shape (**Square, Landscape, Portrait**).

This is handy when selecting images for social media (e.g. Portrait for Instagram Reels and Landscape for YouTube).

To turn off the filter and display all your images, just click on the filter option again – it will toggle on and off each time you press.

Folders

One other useful feature of Midjourney is the ability to organize your images into folders.
   To access this section, make sure you have **Organize** activated on the left-hand side of the screen.

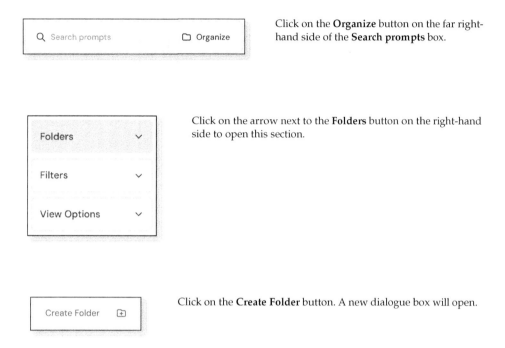

Click on the **Organize** button on the far right-hand side of the **Search prompts** box.

Click on the arrow next to the **Folders** button on the right-hand side to open this section.

Click on the **Create Folder** button. A new dialogue box will open.

There are two choices when creating folders. You can set up a new folder and manually move the images into the folder, or you can use **Smart Folder** to tell Midjourney to collect images with specific characteristics. I will demonstrate both approaches in the next section.

Creating Folders Manually

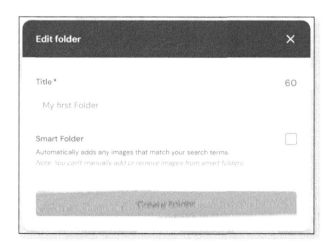

Type a name into the **Title** section of the **Edit Folder** dialogue box.

In my case I used *Café*.

Click on the **Create Folder** button.

The new folder will appear on the right-hand side of your screen in the section **Folders**.

Creating a Folder Using Smart Folders

A quicker way to collect together images in a folder is to use Midjourney's **Smart Folder** option. You can specify search terms and Midjourney will create a folder of all images that used those search terms in the prompt. This will be updated with all images you create in the future that meet the search criteria.

Tick the option **Smart Folder.**

Type in a **Title** for the smart folder (in my case *Cafe*).

In the **Search Terms** box, type a word that is included in the prompt of the images that you want to include in the folder.

You can add multiple terms separated by a comma.

Click on **Create Folder** when you are done.

The new **Smart Folder** will appear at the top of the list in your **Folders** list with a star icon next to it.

Click on the folder name to see the images that are stored in this folder.

If you wish to modify the search terms or to delete the folder, click on the three dots on the right-hand side of the folder name.

If you create a **Smart Folder,** you will not be able to manually add or remove images from that folder. Midjourney will update this folder automatically, adding any new images you create in the future that contain the search word you specified.

Midjourney lists the folders in the order in which they were created – at the time of writing this book there is no way to arrange the list of folders in alphabetical order. This may change, so check out the options that might be available on your version of the software.

Downloading and Saving Multiple Images

As you create each of your images and upscale them you can download and save them one at a time using the instructions provided earlier in this chapter. It is also possible to download multiple images at a time from the **Organize** section of the Midjourney web page. This may be more time efficient, particularly if you are generating a lot of images at one time.

Click on the **Organize** button on the left-hand side of the Midjourney screen.

Before selecting the images, I suggest that you activate the **Filter** options on the right side of the screen to choose the upscaled images only – they will have a higher resolution.

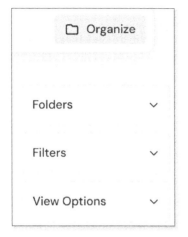

Click on the **Organize** button.

Click on the arrow next to **Filters** to open this section if this is not already open.

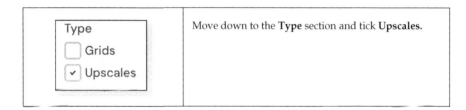

Move down to the **Type** section and tick **Upscales.**

Now that the filter is activated scroll down to the set of images that you would like to download.

To select all the images for a particular day, click on the **+** next to the date – a red tick will appear to show it is selected. Repeat for all of the days that you want to download.

To remove an image from the selection, hold down the **Shift** button of the keyboard and click on the image.

At the bottom of the screen, you will see a new dialogue box pop up showing the number of images that you selected and a **Download** button.

When you click the **Download** button the images that you have selected will be saved to the Downloads folder on your computer as a Zip file. The format of the Zip file name is *midjourney_session_2024_3_30 [0-4]. zip*. The downloading may take a few minutes to finish.

An alternative way to select multiple images is to click outside of the left-hand side of the grid of images that you want to select, hold your mouse down and drag across the images. You will see a pink rectangle as you select. You can then drag down to select multiple rows if you wish.

Let go of the mouse button and you will see a pale pink overlay over the images that are selected (a bit hard to see!). If you want to select images that are not positioned together you can hold your **Shift** button down and click to select individual images.

Explore

On the left-hand side of the Midjourney screen you will see an option labeled **Explore**. When you click on this you will see a grid of images created by other users.

At the top of the **Explore** screen you can choose **Random** (to see a random assortment), **Hot** (for those that others have liked), **Top Day** (recent additions), or **Likes** (images that you have liked). If you see an image that interests you, click on it to enlarge it. This will show you the prompt used to create the image.

In my **Explore** gallery I found this colorful image of a woman with a cup of coffee (see Figure 5.4). This image was created by a user called Savagerus. Don't expect to find the same image on your **Explore** gallery – these images change frequently.

savagerus lw

a woman in sunglasses is looking
at an colorful disk, holding a cup of
coffee, in the style of collage art, high
contrast black and white, urban and
edgy, daz3d, red, layered imagery
with subtle irony, layered portraits

ar 2:3   stylize 250

FIGURE 5.4
Image from the **Explore** Gallery.

Using Other User's Prompts

If you would like to try out the prompt used by someone else, you can click on the **Prompt** button at the bottom right of the enlarged image and this will copy it up into your prompt box.

Use   Image   Style   Prompt

To give Midjourney even more guidance about the image that you want to create, you could also click the **Image** button to add it to the prompt. Using images in the prompt is covered in more detail in Chapter 6.

The image shown in Figure 5.5 is the result that I obtained when I ran the same prompt, including the image.

Midjourney has done a pretty good job of replicating the overall look of the image, without exactly copying any of the details.

This is a great way to learn about different styles or looks that you can apply to other images.

FIGURE 5.5
Output obtained using the prompt copied from **Explore.**

You can experiment by changing words in the prompt before you rerun it.

To get the image shown in Figure 5.6 I replaced *woman in sunglasses* with *man in a cap.*

FIGURE 5.6
Output obtained by changing the original prompt.

Analyzing the prompts used by other people is a great way to learn about the mysterious world of "promptology". The prompt used in this example has some interesting elements that may be worth exploring further to see what impact they have.

For example, it might be interesting to add words from the prompt (e.g. *collage art* or *daz3d*) to other images to see what impact they have. You can also try dropping words from your prompt and rerun to see what you get.

I keep a Word document ready where I paste any interesting images, or styles of artwork, along with the prompt that was used to create them. This has become a great resource for me when I am looking for inspiration. It is fun to try out a particular style on a totally different subject matter to see what result you get.

Combining Other User's Images

The other way that I use the **Explore** gallery in Midjourney is to find images that I can experiment with by combining two or more images to create a new unique style.

I quite liked the two images shown in Figures 5.7 and 5.8 that I found in **Explore**.

I wondered what would happen if I put them both into Midjourney as a two-image prompt.

Detailed instructions for blending two images are provided in Chapter 6.

Figure 5.7 Image 1

Figure 5.8 Image 2

FIGURES 5.7 AND 5.8
Images 1 and 2.

The end result shown in Figure 5.9 is not what I anticipated but it has some interesting elements that I can experiment with further.

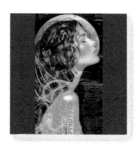

FIGURE 5.9
Output showing the result of blending images shown in Figures 5.7 and 5.8.

Searching Images in Explore

If you are interested in a particular subject (e.g. cafes) and you want to see what other people have produced in **Explore**, click on one of your images, go across to the right-hand side and find the magnifying glass icon above the prompt.

This allows you to search the main Midjourney **Explore** Gallery for other images like yours. This can be helpful when you are learning how to write prompts and are looking for guidance from how others might have achieved their images.

Using my earlier example of an image of bacon and eggs I clicked the magnifying glass icon and the image of a cup of coffee with steam in the shape of woman's face appeared created by a user by the name of *livimel* (see Figure 5.10). This was not something that I would have thought of asking for!

This sent me down a rabbit hole exploring what else I could create with steam – an interesting deviation from my original intention to create an image of bacon and eggs.

FIGURE 5.10
Image found on Explore using the search tool.

An hour later I was still playing – this time producing images of steaming cups with animals in them – see Figure 5.11

Be prepared to go off on tangents, exploring interesting detours – you will often stumble across images that you did not expect!

FIGURE 5.11
Output obtained using a prompt adapted from an image on Explore.

6

Writing Good Prompts

Introduction

Now that you have a basic understanding of how the Midjourney program works we can take a more detailed look at the art and science of writing good prompts. The way in which you write the prompts will have a big impact on the quality and suitability of the images that you receive. Simple prompts will sometimes provide some interesting images, but the real strength of Midjourney is the flexibility, detail, and responsiveness of prompts that you can use to craft an image. Be prepared to experiment and to rerun the image exploring alternative prompts.

Here are a few tips for writing good prompts:

Start with clear objectives but be flexible: Define what you want to achieve with your image. Whether it's a specific scene, object, style, or mood, having a clear goal helps in crafting a precise prompt. Also, be prepared to be flexible with the outcome. Sometimes, you will get an image from Midjourney that is not what you intended but is even more creative.

Be descriptive: Provide detailed descriptions in your prompts. Include specifics about the subject, setting, colors, lighting, and mood. For example, "a serene forest at dusk with soft, warm lighting".

Incorporate styles and influences: If you have a particular artistic style in mind, mention it in your prompt. You can reference art movements, famous artists, or specific techniques.

Use adjectives. Adjectives can greatly influence the outcome. Descriptors like "surreal", "photorealistic", "abstract", or "vibrant" guide Midjourney in generating images that align with your vision.

Refine and rerun: Often, the first result you get from Midjourney might not be perfect. Use it as a starting point, and refine your prompt based on the initial outcome to get closer to your desired image. Experiment with different terms and their position in the prompt.

Understand Midjourney's limitations: Be aware of Midjourney's limitations. Some concepts might be too abstract or complex for it to interpret accurately. If you are requesting an image of something very unusual (e.g., a rare and endangered species of animal) Midjourney may not have had enough exposure to images of the animal you want to create.

If you notice that any of your screens look different to what is shown in the book you can keep up to date with changes to the Midjourney program on my website. You will also find videos showing how you can make the most out of Midjourney.

You can access the website using the link: https://linktr.ee/juliepallant

---

What to Include in a Prompt

Midjourney will generate an image for you, no matter what you include in the prompt. There are, however, a few tricks to get the image that you want (or a reasonable approximation!). There are numerous videos on YouTube giving you recipes for what to include, and what not to include in your prompts.

One approach I have found particularly helpful is that described in a YouTube video by Theoretically Media "A perfect Midjourney prompt formula – great for beginners or advanced users".

His prompt formula contains a number of elements: **medium**, **style/composition**, **scene or object**, **modulate, and commands**.

I will take you through each of these in the sections to follow.

Medium

At the start of the prompt tell Midjourney what medium or format you want. This could be a photograph, painting, line drawing, sketch, watercolor, illustration, poster, and cartoon.

I have included a few examples in Figure 6.1 to show what impact this part of the prompt can have on the image you obtain.

Prompt: detailed pencil line drawing of a mother and her cute little girl, black and white, white background

Prompt: studio photograph of a mother and her cute little girl, black and white, white background

Prompt: abstract artwork of a mother and her cute little girl, black and white, white background

Prompt: cartoon of a mother and her cute little girl, black and white, white background

FIGURE 6.1
Images created in Midjourney specifying different mediums.

Style

Midjourney has been trained to recognize many different art styles (e.g., Art Nouveau) and the work of specific artists (Van Gogh, Monet, Da Vinci). By asking for your image to be "in the style of Monet" for example, Midjourney will change the overall look and feel of your scene to fit this art style.

If you would like to explore multiple styles of the same scene, you can use the following **prompt:** painting of a mother and her cute little girl, in the style of {Monet, Van Gogh, Da Vinci, Art Nouveau}. By including the curly brackets {} you can list the names of any art styles or artists that you would like to create. Midjourney will generate separate prompts for each.

The number of styles you can ask for in one prompt is limited depending on your subscription (Basic = 4, Standard = 10, Pro and Mega = 40). For each of the separate styles, Midjourney will give you a set of four images. In Figure 6.2, I have included examples of the images that I obtained using different styles.

Prompt: painting of a mother and her cute little girl, in the style of DaVinci

Prompt: painting of a mother and her cute little girl, in the style of Art Nouveau

Prompt: painting of a mother and her cute little girl, in the style of Monet

Prompt: painting of a mother and her cute little girl, in the style of Van Gogh

FIGURE 6.2
Images created in Midjourney specifying different art styles.

Many of us using Midjourney to generate art have an ethical concern about using the name and style of living artists as part of a prompt. AI does not copy existing artworks, but instead it analyses the style and applies it to a scene to create a new unique piece of work. Despite this I don't feel comfortable "copying" the style of living artists who have spent many years developing their own unique looks and are trying to earn a living from their work. This is something that you will need to think about and decide how you feel about the issue.

Composition

In this part of the prompt, you can tell Midjourney the camera angle or shot type you want. Possibilities include wide-angle, close-up, satellite, overhead, head and shoulders, full body, low angle, and eye level (see Figure 6.3).

Prompt: photograph of a mother and her cute little girl, low angle shot

Prompt: photograph of a mother and her cute little girl, close-up shot

Prompt: photograph of a mother and her cute little girl, overhead shot

Prompt: photograph of a mother and her cute little girl, full body shot

FIGURE 6.3
Images created in Midjourney specifying different camera angles and shot types.

Scene

The next part of the prompt is where you describe the elements that you want in a scene. It can be as simple as "a mother and cute little girl" as I have used in the prompt of the earlier image, or as detailed as a full movie scene where you specify the subject, actions, props, lighting, and location details.

From Version 6 in Midjourney onwards it is possible to write full descriptions of the image that you want, using normal sentence structure (as if you were describing the image in a conversation with a friend). Break your instructions into logical sentences, explaining clearly what you want to see in the image.

Describe the main subject of your image, what they are wearing, where they are positioned, and in what direction they are looking. Provide information about the setting, the background, the lighting, and the overall mood of the image. One of the instructions that you might find helpful to include is whether your subject is facing the camera or looking away (see Figure 6.4).

Prompt: photograph of a woman wearing long white flowing dress. She is standing on a hilltop, looking away out over the vast expanse of the universe, the stars, milky way and a bright white light in the distance. The mood of the image is spiritual, magical, mystical, uplifting.

Prompt: photograph of a father and daughter, show their full bodies walking on a beach towards the camera. They are holding hands. The daughter is 6 years of age with long hair blowing in the breeze. The beach background is blurred with a shallow depth of field. The mood is fun, relaxing.

FIGURE 6.4
Images created in Midjourney specifying different scenes.

Important: It is important to note that Midjourney pays more attention to those elements or keywords listed early in your prompt, compared with those listed later. If you are not getting the results that you want, try rearranging the order of the terms. Keep your prompts short and to the point – don't include a lot of unnecessary waffle – this will just confuse Midjourney.

When you are looking through the images and prompts on **Explore** that others have created, don't assume that they are good prompts. There are many bad prompts where people have included a lot of unnecessary and often contradictory information.

Modulate

You can use additional descriptive terms in the prompt to give Midjourney information about the tone or feeling of the image that you want. These modulating terms can produce quite dramatic results.

In the previous section I used additional descriptive terms in the first prompt of the woman looking out over the universe. These included "spiritual, magical, mystical, uplifting". These helped to create the mood of the image. If, on the other hand, you wanted a darker, more sinister tone (e.g., for a crime novel cover) you could include words such as dark, moody, and mysterious in the prompt (see examples shown in Figure 6.5).

Prompt: happy young girl skipping away through a meadow of flowers, bright sunshine in the background, wide angle image showing her full body facing away into the distance, inspiring, uplifting, beautiful.

Prompt: crime novel book cover, large male untidy detective in a coat, walking away, a long way down a dark deserted street with street-lamps, dark, moody, mysterious, threatening

FIGURE 6.5
Images created in Midjourney specifying different moods.

You can also specify words relating to the season (e.g. summer, winter, autumn, spring) – this will have an impact on the colors and textures of the image, the clothes that people are wearing, and the locations that Midjourney chooses (see Figure 6.6).

Prompt: photograph of a young couple in love walking hand in hand, **summer**

Prompt: photograph of a young couple in love walking hand in hand, **winter**

Prompt: photograph of a young couple in love walking hand in hand, **autumn**

Prompt: photograph of a young couple in love walking hand in hand, **spring**

FIGURE 6.6
Images created in Midjourney specifying different seasons.

Additional Tips on Writing Prompts

In the Midjourney documentation, there are a few additional tips about writing prompts that you might want to consider. In the Prompting Notes section of the documentation there is an explanation of the impact that prompt length has on the images that you will obtain:

> Prompts can be simple. A single word or emoji will work. However, short prompts rely on Midjourney's default style, allowing it to fill in any unspecified details creatively. Include any element that is important to you in your prompt. Fewer details mean more variety, but less control.
> *Midjourney documentation: https://docs.midjourney.com/docs/prompts-2*

It includes a list of details that you could consider adding to your prompt to guide Midjourney:

Subject: person, animal, character, location, object
Medium: photo, painting, illustration, sculpture, doodle, tapestry
Environment: indoors, outdoors, on the moon, underwater, in the city
Lighting: soft, ambient, overcast, neon, studio lights
Color: vibrant, muted, bright, monochromatic, colorful, black and white, pastel
Mood: sedate, calm, raucous, energetic
Composition: portrait, headshot, closeup, birds-eye view
Midjourney documentation: https://docs.midjourney.com/docs/prompts-2

It is not compulsory to add this level of detail to each image that you generate, however, it can be helpful when you have a specific goal in mind.

Requesting Text in an Image

To request text in an image, you need to write the prompt with words of the text in double quotation marks " ". I wanted to make a greeting card with the words Happy New Year in the center.

My prompt was:

Prompt: "Happy New Year" written in the centre of gold fireworks on dark blue background with bokeh on New Year's Eve, Abstract background --ar 2:3

The result is shown in Figure 6.7.

FIGURE 6.7
Requesting **Text** in a Midjourney prompt.

Adding text to an image is a relatively new feature for Midjourney and tends to be hit and miss. You can keep rerunning the prompt to see if it will behave, but I prefer to have control over this process, so I generate the background in Midjourney and open the image in Adobe Photoshop, and add the extra text that I want.

This gives you much more control over the font, size, color, and position of the text.

You will notice that the prompt has an extra bit on the end --ar 2:3. This tells Midjourney that I want the image to be portrait orientation and with the aspect ratio of 2:3 (Width: Height). This is covered in more detail in the next section.

Adding Extra Commands to a Prompt

Midjourney offers a number of additional controls that allow you to craft and customize the images that it generates for you. Midjourney refers to these as "parameters". These are optional but can be very helpful in obtaining the results that you want.

Please note that not all these parameters work with all versions of the program. Midjourney frequently makes changes and updates so some of the material may have changed if you are using a later version than version 6 that is shown here.

To keep up to date you might like to refer to the Midjourney Help menu: https://docs.midjourney. com/docs/parameter-list. A useful YouTube video on the topic is "Midjourney control for beginners and advanced users" by Theoretically Media.

There are two ways to access these additional commands.

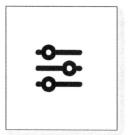

The first approach is to click on the setting icon on the right hand side of the prompt box and to use the sliders provided.

The second approach is to add additional commands to the end of the prompt.

In the sections below, I will take you on a tour of the various options available showing how to use both approaches.

Aspect Ratio

The default aspect ratio (or shape) generated by Midjourney is a square that has an aspect ratio of 1:1 (equal height and width). If the square shape suits you, then you don't need to do anything.

If, however, you want your image to be a rectangle, then you can specify the proportion or aspect ratio. The aspect ratio of images generated by a professional Canon or Nikon camera is 2:3. The first number refers to the width and the second number is the height. The shape of an image on television or YouTube is 16:9.

In Midjourney you can choose whichever aspect ratio suits your image or your needs, using any values. You might want to consider how and where you will be using the image and adjust accordingly.

In Figure 6.8, I show two images I created in Midjourney for greeting cards. In the first image, I wanted a portrait orientation, so I chose to use a 3:4 ratio to suit the card design. For the second image, I wanted a landscape orientation, so I requested an aspect ratio of 4:3.

Prompt: a shaggy white cavoodle cute dog wearing sunglasses, summer themed background, the words "Get Well Soon" written in bold letters, coloured painting --ar 3:4

Prompt: Australian grevillea flowers, artistic, beautiful --v 4, --ar 4:3

FIGURE 6.8
Images created in Midjourney for greeting cards using different **Aspect Ratios**.

There are two ways to tell Midjourney the aspect ratio that you want to use. The first way is to press the settings icon at the right-hand side of the prompt box.

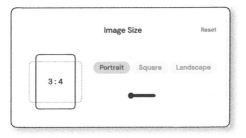

In the section labeled **Image Size** move the slider to the left to create a **Portrait**-oriented image or to the right to specify **Landscape** orientation.

All future images will use the new aspect ratio you specified until you change it again.

The second way to specify the aspect ratio is to type an extra command at the end of your prompt. Go to the end of your prompt in the prompt box and type two hyphens followed by the ratio that you want to use:

--ar 3:4 or **--ar 4:3**   Just to clarify, this is: hyphen hypen ar space 3 colon 4.

Some computers will combine the 2 short hyphens into one longer em dash – don't panic if this happens, Midjourney accepts both.

The advantage of using this second approach to specifying the aspect ratio is that it only applies to the specific prompt that you add it to. This means you can choose which aspect ratio you want to use for each prompt rather than setting a default value that applies to all future prompts, as in the case of method 1. Even if you have set an aspect ratio using the sliders, any ratio you specify in the prompt will take precedence.

You can specify any aspect ratio you would like. I have listed some of the more commonly used aspect ratios in Table 6.1.

TABLE 6.1
Commonly Used Aspect Ratios

Instagram posts grid and profile picture	1:1
Instagram Stories and Reels (vertical)	9:16
YouTube video (horizontal)	16:9
Print on A4 paper	210:297
Print as greeting card A4 in quarters	114:162

Mode

Midjourney images tend to have a particular look or style to them by default. If you want your images to look more realistic or photographic, you can reduce the amount of stylizing applied by Midjourney. This is done by changing the **Mode** to **Raw**. There are two ways to do this.

The first way is to open the Settings icon on the right of the prompt box.

Go to the **Model** section and down to **Mode**.

Click on **Raw**.

This option will remain in place for all subsequent image generations until you change it.

The alternative method for selecting **Raw** is to type **--style raw** to the end of your prompt in the prompt box.

Prompt: bird sitting on a branch --style raw

In the example shown in Figure 6.9, I used the same prompt, with **Standard** mode (left) and **Raw** mode (on the right).

Prompt: bird sitting on a branch   **Prompt**: bird sitting on a branch –style raw

FIGURE 6.9
Images created in Midjourney showing the impact of the **Standard** vs **Raw** mode.

Specifying the style as **Raw** results in bird images that look more realistic and photographic than the **Standard** default which are more painterly. Depending on the subject matter of your image I suggest that you experiment with using both the **Raw** and **Standard** options to see what works best for your image.

Version

In the **Model** section there is a drop-down box titled **Version** – this refers to the version of Midjourney. The most up to date version for me is Version 6.1. Depending on when you are reading this book the version number is likely to be higher as Midjourney regularly releases updates with new features.

Each version of the program has a different "look" so you might want to explore which version suits your particular purpose. I like to try using versions 5.1 and 5.2 when creating artwork as I find it gives a softer, more "painterly" effects, whereas Version 6.1 is much better at photographic and realistic images.

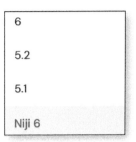

If you scroll further down in the **Version** menu you will also see another option: **Niji 6.**

Niji is a specialized version that creates images with an anime style, as shown in Figure 6.10.

Prompt: anime young girl surrounded by cherry blossoms

Prompt: anime girl with long black straight hair

FIGURE 6.10
Images created in Midjourney using the **Niji 6** version.

You can also access this version by adding **--niji 6** at the end of the prompt.

In the set of images in Figure 6.11, I illustrate the impact of changing the versions by using the same prompt each time, but changing the version: **niji 6, v 6, v 5.2, v 4.**

Prompt: girl wearing school uniform --niji 6   **Prompt**: girl wearing school uniform --v 6

Prompt: girl wearing school unform --v 5.2   **Prompt**: girl wearing school uniform --v 4

FIGURE 6 11

Examples of images created in Midjourney using different version numbers.

When working with different versions of Midjourney, the available options to upscale or vary images will be different. More options are available with the later versions, so I recommend you start with these first.

Important: if you decide to experiment with different version numbers in your Settings, remember to set it back to the most recent version when you have finished.

Speed

Under the tools menu there is a **More Options** section. Here you can set your speed to **Relax, Fast,** and **Turbo**.

The availability of these settings depends on which subscription plan you have.

If you have a **Standard** plan (currently US$30/month), you have an unlimited number of hours that you can use if you set the speed to **Relax**, however, your **Fast** hours are capped at 15hrs/month (this value may change).

On the **Standard** plan, you can choose to swap between **Fast** (when you are in a hurry) and **Slow** (when you are prepared to wait). This option is not available if you are on the **Basic Plan**.

Stylization

The **Stylize** slider influences how strongly Midjourney applies its default styling to produce images. You can choose a value from 0 to 1000 to control the strength. Low stylize values produce images more closely aligned with your prompt. High stylize values create more artistic images, which may vary from what you originally asked for, but could give some interesting results.

To access **Stylize** click on the Settings button on the right-hand side of the prompt **box**.

Move the slider to the left to lower the value and to the right to increase the value.

Hover your mouse over the slider and the value will appear. As a guideline: low = 50, medium = 100 (default value), high = 250, very high = 750.

An alternative method to adjust the stylization is to go to the end of your prompt and type:

--stylize *(or **--s**)* and type a value between 0 to 1000

To experiment, I generated two prompts, one using the stylized value of 0 and the other using the value of 1000. I used the shortened version of command **--s** (see Figure 6.12 for the results).

Prompt: older woman with a flower in her hair at an outdoor party --s 0

Prompt: older woman with a flower in her hair at an outdoor party --s 1000

FIGURE 6.12
Images created in Midjourney with variations to the **Stylize** value.

In this example the "low stylize" image (on the left) is consistent with the prompt, while the "high stylize" version included women who did not appear to fit the "older woman" part of the prompt. There is also a difference in the look of the two images with the "low stylize" image having a raw photographic look, compared to the more glamorized "high stylize" image on the right.

When generating your own prompts, you might want to play around with different **Stylization** values to see what best suits your needs. To speed this process up you can ask Midjourney to generate multiple prompts, varying the stylize values. This short cut is called **Permutations** and will be covered in more detail later in this chapter.

Please note: this **Permutations** option is not available if you are on the Basic subscription plan (US$10/month). You must have at least a **Standard** subscription and you need to set your **Speed** to **Fast** (see the previous **Speed** section).

To run multiple commands within a single prompt, add the following command to the end of your prompt:

--s {50,100,250,750}

The values between the curly brackets {} are the stylize values you want to generate. Instead of writing four separate prompts, you just provide one and Midjourney will write and run the four separate prompts for you.

Prompt: older woman with a flower in her hair at an outdoor party, --s {50,100,250,750}

Midjourney would then break this into four separate prompts:

older woman with a flower in her hair at an outdoor party --s 50
older woman with a flower in her hair at an outdoor party --s 100
older woman with a flower in her hair at an outdoor party --s 250
older woman with a flower in her hair at an outdoor party --s 750

It would then run each of these prompts separately and provide you with a grid of four images for each prompt.

Weirdness

The **Weirdness** slider gives you the chance to let your hair down and live dangerously!

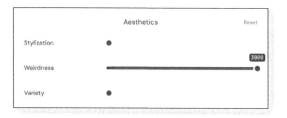

Values can range from 0 to 3000, with high values offering quirky and off-beat versions of your image

The default value is 0 but you can experiment by trying out different values to see what effect it has. In the example shown in Figure 6.13, I used a value of 0 to obtain the image on the left, and when I used a value of 3000, I obtained the image on the right.

Prompt: elderly couple dressed in eye catching outfits for fancy dress night, realistic, very detailed high quality image, shot by a famous professional photographer for a fashion magazine --style raw --stylize 0 --weird 0

Prompt: elderly couple dressed in eye catching outfits for fancy dress night, realistic, very detailed high quality image, shot by a famous professional photographer for a fashion magazine --style raw --stylize 0 --weird 3000

FIGURE 6.13
Images created in Midjourney with variations to the **Weirdness** value.

Variety

The **Variety** slider changes how varied the four images that Midjourney generates from a prompt will be. In previous versions of Midjourney on Discord this was known as **Chaos**.

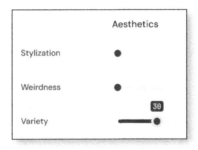

Variety values can range from 0 to 100. Higher values will produce a mix of images that are quite different to one another. The default is 0.

- If you are starting out and don't quite know what you want your image to look like I suggest that you use a higher variety value of 100. This will give you lots of different ideas to start with.
- As you become clearer on what you want, reduce your value down to a lower value. This will keep some consistency in the images that Midjourney produces for you.

Whatever value you set the **Variety** slider it will be used for all subsequent image generations until you change it.

An alternative way to access this feature is to type a command at the end of the **prompt**:

--chaos 100 *(or --c 100).*

Using this approach has the advantage of only affecting this particular image generation.

To demonstrate the use of the **Variety** slider I have run the **prompt**: Photo of the Eiffel Tower, first using a variety value of 0, and then again with the value of 100. In Figure 6.14 variety is referred to as chaos (Midjourney only recently changed the name – this confusing mix of terminology is likely to be fixed in later versions of the program).

Prompt: photo of the Eiffel Tower –chaos 0   **Prompt**: photo of the Eiffel Tower –chaos 100

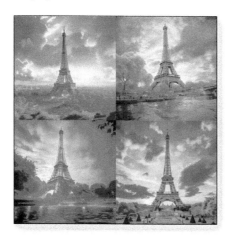 

FIGURE 6.14

Images created in Midjourney with variations to the **Variety** value.

There is a lot more variability across the four images when the **Variety** slider is set to 100 (right image), than when the value is set to 0 (left image).

Specifying What You Don't Want in an Image

If there is something you don't want in your image you can try using the **--no** command at the end of the prompt, specifying what you don't want included. In Figure 6.15, I asked for a: **photograph of a cafe --no people, cars**

Prompt: photograph of a cafe, --no people, cars   **Prompt**: photograph of a café --no people, cars

FIGURE 6.15
Results of a prompt requesting no people or cars.

Midjourney did a great job resisting the urge to put people into my cafe images. This was probably a difficult task for Midjourney as I suspect most of the images of cafes that it was originally trained on would have had people in them. Warning – It does not always work this well!

Using Images in a Prompt

Midjourney allows you to upload one or more images to be used as inspiration to create a new image. You can use images you have taken yourself, saved from the web, or an image generated by Midjourney. They need to have been saved onto your computer. Additional text can then be added to the prompt to describe the content that you want.

Be warned – Midjourney will not copy the image exactly but will re-imagine it so the results will differ (in some cases quite substantially) from the original. At this point in time (June 2024) Midjourney is not a good tool if you want to take an image of a person and to insert it into a background. The new image may look a bit like the original person, but in my experience, it often gets it very wrong!

Including images in prompts can be used to generate some quite creative outcomes, but lots of experimenting will be required if you have a particular outcome in mind. Keep an open mind – you might find some new more creative images that you would have never considered!

In the example to follow I demonstrate how I use an image I had previously generated in Midjourney with the prompt "**abstract ethereal graphic design background**". This image had been upscaled and downloaded to my computer (see Figure 6.16).

Prompt: abstract ethereal graphic design background

FIGURE 6.16
Image used in a prompt.

Using a Single Image in the Prompt

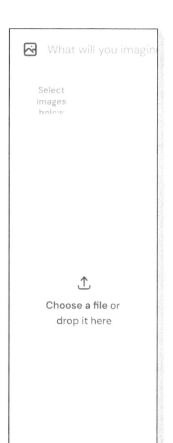

Click on the **image icon** at the front of the prompt box.

This will open a drop-down box asking you to **Choose a file or drop it here**.

Navigate to the location of your image on your computer and click **Open**.

This will upload the image to the area just below the prompt box.

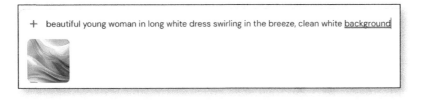

With the image uploaded you now need to add some words to the prompt.

When using only a single image Midjourney requires you to add a text prompt as well.

If you use two or more images, a text prompt is optional.

The prompt I used was:

Prompt: beautiful young woman in long white dress swirling in the breeze, clean white background

Press **Enter** on the keyboard to run the prompt.

The result I obtained by using the image and the word prompt is shown in Figure 6.17.

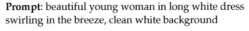

Prompt: beautiful young woman in long white dress swirling in the breeze, clean white background

FIGURE 6.17
Image obtained using a single image + word prompt in Midjourney.

I found this approach a great way to experiment with applying different backgrounds. The results that you get can be quite unexpected, which is one of the things I love about Midjourney.

Using Multiple Images in the Prompt

You are not limited to using only one image in a prompt – you can upload up to five images for Midjourney to combine. When using only one image you must add an additional text prompt, but when you use two or more images in your prompt no additional text is required, but you can choose to add it if you wish.

Load your images following the procedure described in the previous section but hold the **Ctrl** key down as you select multiple images to bring them up to the prompt box

In Figure 6.18, I show the results of combining the first two images, without any additional text prompt, to create the third image.

Image 1

Image 2

Final result of Image 1 and Image 2 combined

FIGURE 6.18
Result obtained by combining two images in a prompt, without added text.

In the next section we will explore some more advanced techniques that you can apply when using images as part of your prompts. These can have a big impact on the final look of your image.

Image Weights

If you are using an image, in addition to a text prompt, you can apply what is known as an **image weight**. This tells Midjourney how important you want the uploaded image to be, in comparison with the text part of the prompt.

The default value is 1 (equal contribution of both the text and image). Weight values can range from 0 to 3 for Version 6, and from 0 to 2 for Version 5.

- If you want the generated image to be very similar to the image you have uploaded, (to have a greater weight), add this command to the end of your **prompt**: --iw 3 (for Version 6) or --iw 2 (for Version 5)
- If you want the **text** part of the prompt to contribute more and the **image** part to be less important, use the image weight of **--iw .5**

In the example shown in Figure 6.19, I used an image I found on **Explore** created by username *costa3388*.

Prompt: portrait of a beautiful woman, black and white, pencil drawing, sketch

FIGURE 6.19
Image and prompt obtained from the **Explore** gallery.

Shown Figure 6.20 are the results when I used the same text and image prompt to the original, but added an image weight to the end of the **prompt**: --iw 3.

Prompt: portrait of a beautiful woman, black and white, pencil drawing, sketch --iw 3

FIGURE 6.20
Set of four images obtained using the command **--iw 3**.

Consistent with the high value for the image weighting, the four images were very similar to the original image from **Explore**.

I then changed the image weight to **--iw .5** which told Midjourney I did not want the image to be very influential (see Figure 6.21).

Prompt: portrait of a beautiful woman, black and white, pencil drawing, sketch --iw .5

FIGURE 6.21
Set of four images obtained using the command --**iw .5**.

Using the lower image weight of .5, the set of four images I obtained were quite different to the original image.

Style Reference

If you find an image that you like the overall look or style of and want to apply this to other images you can use a *style reference*.

Style references give you the ability to copy the style of an existing image and to apply it to new images generated in Midjourney. This is similar to using an image in a prompt (described earlier in this chapter), but focuses solely on the style, allowing you the flexibility to request another character, setting, or theme for your image.

In this next example I found an image of a very colorful cat that I liked on **Explore** (from frida2765) and I wanted to apply this colorful style to other subjects. I dragged this image (see Figure 6.22) from the **Explore** gallery up into the prompt box.

FIGURE 6.22
Image from the **Explore** gallery.

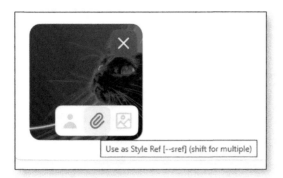

I moved my cursor over the bottom right of the image until I saw three little icons appear. I clicked on the middle icon (a paperclip) which is the **Style Reference**.

I copied the original prompt (*abstract dadaist graphical poster futurism feat beautiful black cat*) up into the prompt box.

I removed *the black cat* and replaced it with a *beautiful woman wearing sunglasses.*
The image I obtained is shown in Figure 6.23.

Prompt: abstract dadaist graphical poster futurism feat beautiful

FIGURE 6.23
Output from Midjourney using a **Style Reference**.

To increase the influence of the style, you can apply a **style weight** which tells Midjourney that you want the new image to be very similar to the reference image.
   To do this you add an extra command on the end of the written prompt in the prompt box: **--sw** (followed by a number from 0 to 1000)
   Style weight values range from 0 to 1000, with a default value of 100, which is applied if you don't specify another value. High values apply the style heavily, while low values decrease its influence.
   You can only apply a style weight when you have uploaded an image to the prompt box, and you have clicked on the **Style Ref** button (paperclip icon).
   In the next example I experimented by adding the maximum style weight by typing **--sw 1000** at the end of the prompt, using the original cat image set to **Style Reference**.

Prompt: abstract dadaist graphical poster futurism featuring beautiful woman wearing sunglasses --sw 1000

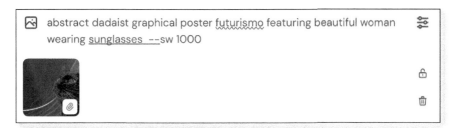

The resulting image below matched the style of the original cat image well, with very similar colors, image composition, and position of the subject. Using this higher weighting value certainly resulted in a better match than the first attempt where I did not specify a weight.

FIGURE 6.24
Output from Midjourney.

Character Reference

Artists wanting to create a consistent character to use across a series of images (e.g., children's book) have been very frustrated by Midjourney's tendency to change facial features each time a new image is generated. This is slowly improving as time goes on, but at this time (August 2024) it is still not very reliable.

Here are a few ways that you can improve your chances of getting consistent characters. The instructions provided are based on Version 6, so if you are using a later version of Midjourney keep an eye out for alternative ways to achieve consistency. The **Character Reference** feature does not work with earlier versions of Midjourney so make sure Version 6 or higher is selected in the Settings menu.

Start by creating a character in Midjourney that you want to use across multiple settings. I used the prompt shown below:

Prompt: Watercolour cartoon style children's book illustration. A young boy wearing brown shorts and a white shirt. He is sitting on a chair eating his lunch. He has short brown hair.

Four images were generated and I chose the one shown in Figure 6.25 to work with:

FIGURE 6.25
One of the four images output from Midjourney.

To use this as a character reference I dragged and dropped it up into the prompt box.

If you hover your mouse over the bottom right of the thumbnail image, you will see three gray icons appear.

The first icon (shaped like a person's head) is the **Character Reference**.

I clicked on this icon so that it was highlighted at the bottom of the image thumbnail.

In the prompt box I changed the prompt to:

Prompt: Watercolour cartoon style children's book illustration. A young boy wearing brown shorts and a white shirt. He is sitting on a chair reading a book. He has short brown hair.

The new image is shown in Figure 6.26.

It is not an exact copy of the boy, but it is a reasonable approximation

FIGURE 6.26
Output from Midjourney after changing the prompt.

I then repeated the same process to create more images, changing the prompt each time to obtain images of the boy riding a bike and walking his dog (see Figure 6.27).

FIGURE 6.27
Additional images obtained by adapting the original prompt.

In the previous example I wanted my character to look the same, and be wearing the same clothes, across all the settings. If, however, you want to change your character's clothes, you need to add a **Character Weight** to the end of your prompt. This takes the form: **--cw** followed by a value from 0 to 100.

Adding the command **--cw 0** will replicate the face, but not the clothes or accessories, from the reference image. Therefore, if you want to your character to change clothes you should add **--cw 0** to the end of your prompt.

The default value of 100 is applied when you don't specify a value. Midjourney will use the same face, hair, and clothes as present in the original reference image. You may need to experiment with other values to achieve the effect that you want.

In the example here I added **--cw 0** to the end of the prompt. I also changed the prompt, requesting a different colored shirt and a different location.

Prompt: Watercolour cartoon style children's book illustration. A young boy wearing a red and white striped shirt. He is at the beach eating an ice-cream. He has short brown hair --cw 0

+   Watercolor cartoon style children's book illustration. A young boy wearing a red and white striped shirt. He is at the beach eating an icecream . He has short brown hair --chaos 20 --ar 2:3 --style raw --stylize 0 --cw 0

The result of the revised prompt is shown in Figure 6.28.

Midjourney has changed the boy's shirt to stripes and it has put him at the beach, while still retaining the same boy's face and hair.

FIGURE 6.28
Output from Midjourney after applying a character weight.

If you wish to use an image as both a **Character Reference** and a **Style Reference** (see the previous sections) hold the **Shift** button down on your keyboard and click on both icons at the bottom of the image.

Warning: These features are still under development and may not work as you expect. It may take a bit of experimenting, trying different weight values, to see if you can improve the result. Midjourney still struggles with consistency with photographic, rather than illustrative images, but hopefully this will improve over time.

Head Swap

One of the features that many of us would love to see included in the Midjourney program is the ability to head-swap a photo of a person directly into a scene generated in Midjourney. Unfortunately, as of June 2024, there is no direct way to achieve this reliably in the program.

Sometimes the **Character Reference** feature in Midjourney will give you a reasonable outcome, but it is still quite hit and miss. In case you want to try it for yourself I will take you through the steps in an example below.

Start by generating an image of a person in the setting that you desire. In my case I used the following prompt:

Prompt: Scottish castle as a background for a head and shoulders portrait of a scottish warrior

I have used a very simple prompt as an example however I would encourage you to describe the scene in a lot more detail so that Midjourney understands the look you are after.

In Figure 6.29 one of the images that Midjourney provided is shown – I have clicked on the image and pressed the **Upscale** button.

FIGURE 6.29
Output from Midjourney.

I clicked on both the **Image** and **Prompt** buttons in the **Use** section of the tools on the bottom right of the image.

This moved the prompt and image up to the prompt box.

I also added two photographic head-shots that I had of a friend to the prompt box. You can use one or more images to show your person from different angles.

For the two head-shots I clicked on the **Character Reference** icons below the images to tell Midjourney to use this information as the character reference.

At the end of the prompt, I added the command **--cw 0** to tell Midjourney to only use the face, and not the hair, clothes, or background, of the **Character Reference** images.

The image that Midjourney created for me is shown in Figure 6.30.

I wasn't happy with the colors in the image, so I converted it to black and white in Photoshop.

FIGURE 6.30
Midjourney image using character reference **--cw 0**.

The final edited image is shown in Figure 6.31.

FIGURE 6.31
Conversion of Midjourney image to black and white.

At this point in time head-swapping is not a reliable feature in Midjourney, although keep an eye out for developments! In the meantime, there are many other head swapping programs and apps available that you might like to explore. For a review of head swapping tools go to: www.unite.ai/best-ai-face-swap-tools/

Create Multiple Images of a Character

Another way to tackle the problem of creating consistent characters for a comic or children's book is to request a character sheet of multiple views of the same character. To achieve this, you should use words such as "sheet of many poses" or "consistent character from many angles" in the prompt.

In Figure 6.32, I provide an example of the prompt that I used to create a set of consistent characters and the output I obtained from Midjourney.

Prompt: cartoon style character, young girl with brown hair, sheet of many poses, consistent character from many angles

FIGURE 6.32
Character sheet generated by Midjourney.

If you use this approach, you will need to have good Photoshop skills to composite the character into different background scenes generated separately in Midjourney.

Describe

Midjourney has recently added a feature, **Describe,** which will analyze an image you upload and suggest descriptions that you could use in a prompt to create something similar. Images that you upload must be less than 10 MB in size.

I was intrigued with an image that I found online and wanted to see what Midjourney would suggest as a prompt to recreate something similar.

First you need to save the image on your computer. Click the **icon** at the front of the prompt box, navigate to where your image is located, select it, and click **Open**. The image will appear in an area below the prompt box.

Position your cursor over the uploaded image and you will see a lowercase i – click on it, and a new window will appear.

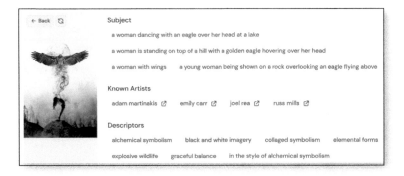

Midjourney provides you with descriptive terms for the **Subject**, any **Known Artists** that have a similar style, and **Descriptors** that could be included in the prompt. Click on any terms you want to use, and they will appear in the prompt box.

Figure 6.33 shows the image that Midjourney produced for me when I used the information provided by **Describe**.

FIGURE 6.33
Output after using **Describe**.

Permutations

Permutations can speed up your prompting by allowing you to quickly generate variations of a prompt within a single command. For example, if you wanted separate photographs of a cute puppy and a cute kitten sitting in a box you could use the prompt shown below:

Prompt: photograph of cute funny {puppy, kitten} sitting in a box, golden sunlight coming from behind.

A separate grid of images will be produced for each of the terms in the curly brackets {}. In this case, a puppy and a kitten.

There is a limit to the number of prompts that can be requested from a single permutation prompt, depending on your subscription plan:

- 4 prompts for **Basic** subscribers
- 10 prompts for **Standard** subscribers
- 40 prompts for **Pro** and **Mega** subscribers

The results of the two prompts that Midjourney created are shown in Figure 6.34 (just in case you needed a dose of cuteness!).

Prompt: photograph of cute funny puppy sitting in a box, golden sunlight coming from behind

Prompt: photograph of cute funny kitten sitting in a box, golden sunlight coming from behind

FIGURE 6.34
Output from {kitten, puppy} **Permutations** in Midjourney.

This technique can also be used to request multiple images based on other descriptors. For example, to experiment with images of a model in different colored dresses you could use the following prompt:

Prompt: photograph of a beautiful young fashion model wearing a {white, blue} dress

Midjourney will write two separate prompts for you, varying the color of the dress in each prompt (see Figure 6.35). For each of these prompts four images will be generated.

Prompt: photograph of a beautiful young fashion model wearing a white dress

Prompt: photograph of a beautiful young fashion model wearing a blue dress

FIGURE 6.35
Output from {white, blue} **Permutations** in Midjourney.

For photographers or models this is a great way to try out different looks for potential photoshoots and to create mood boards and shot lists.

Repeat

The other feature in Midjourney that can save you some time is the **Repeat** function. This tells Midjourney to run the same prompt multiple times so that you have more images to choose from.

To use **Repeat** you write your prompt in the prompt box and then at the end you add: **--repeat** followed by a number to indicate how many times you want it repeated. This command can be shortened to **--r**.

In the example below I asked Midjourney to rerun the prompt 3 times, with 4 choices each time, giving a total of 12 images.

Prompt: girl wearing a red dress, --r 3

The result that I obtained is shown in Figure 6.36.

Prompt: girl wearing a red dress, --r 3

FIGURE 6.36
Output from **Repeat** in **Midjourney**.

There are limitations on the values that you can use with the **Repeat** command, depending on your subscription

- For a **Basic** subscription you can use values 2–4
- For a **Standard** subscription you can use values 2–10
- For **Pro** and **Mega** subscriptions, you can use values 2–40

Multi-Prompts

When you are creating a prompt that includes two or more components it is usually enough to include a comma between the two components for Midjourney to consider them separately. If this does not work you can you can add a set of double colons:: to separate the two parts – this tells Midjourney to consider each part of the prompt separately.

The example that Midjourney uses in their documentation is:

Prompt: space::ship

If you use the double colon to separate the parts, you can also add a number immediately after the double colon to assign a weight to the component – that is to tell Midjourney how important it is to you.

In the example below the value 2 after the :: tells Midjourney that "space" is twice as important to "ship" and that it should be the main focus of the image. Image weight values range from 0 to 3 for Version 6 of the program and from 0 to 2 for Version 5.

Prompt: space::2 ship

I have to admit I have not found this multi-prompt feature very helpful, but you might like to experiment with your own images to see what difference it makes.

Tile

Another feature of Midjourney that graphic designers might find useful is the ability to generate an image that can be repeated seamlessly to create a continuous pattern. These are a popular item online for creating fabrics, clothing, papers, notebooks, wallpaper, etc.

At the time of writing this book this **Tile** feature was not available as a tick box or slider in the Midjourney Settings, instead you need to add an extra command to the end of your prompt.

 a pattern of colourful autumn leaves in watercolour --tile

Describe the pattern that you want and add **--tile** at the end of the prompt.

The result I obtained is shown in Figure 6.37.

Prompt: a pattern of colourful autumn leaves in watercolour –**tile**

FIGURE 6.37
Output from **Tile** in Midjourney.

The Midjourney documentation (available at https://docs.midjourney.com/docs) suggests testing how well your tile image will create a seamless pattern using a **Seamless Texture Checker** at www.pycheung.com/checker/ (this is free to use).

Open the **Seamless Texture Checker** and click on the **File** button. You can then drag and drop your image from the Midjourney window into the Checker window.

In the window you will be able to see the tiled version of your image.

The program will show your pattern repeated multiple times in all directions. Use the slider bar at the top of the Checker screen to zoom out to see how well your pattern repeats.

If you are happy with the repeating pattern, click on the download button on the far right of the **Seamless Texture Checker tool** bar.

The file will be saved to your download folder as *seamlesscheck1.png*. Rename it and save it on your computer.

This tile technique works well across many different types of images. In Figure 6.38, I have included another example using cat icons (yes, another cat image – I cannot help myself!).

Prompt: pattern of cute cartoon watercolour illustrations
of different shaped cats in warm tones --**tile**

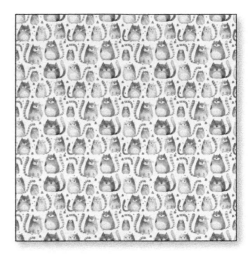

FIGURE 6.38
Example of image output from Midjourney and tiled version from Seamless Texture Checker.

7

Further Inspiration

Introduction

If you have followed along with the training examples included in the book you should now have a good understanding of how to create images in Midjourney. In this final chapter, the focus shifts to how you can make use of the images that you create. I share with you examples of some Midjourney users whose work might inspire you to explore the diverse range of possibilities available for AI-generated art.

Case Studies of Midjourney Users

In this section, I provide a number of case studies showing the different ways that people have chosen to use the Midjourney program as a creative tool. For some, it is part of their professional workflow; for others, it is a creative tool for their own enjoyment. I chose to include a range of different people to feature, from different backgrounds, and who are using AI images in different ways.

For each of the creators featured in this section I sent them a questionnaire asking them about their work, views on AI, and for any tips or hints for people just starting out. With some I was also able to follow up with Zoom interviews and have included their words of wisdom here.

Damien Bredberg: Photographer

Damien Bredberg is a photographer working in the areas of advertising, commercial, property, corporate, architectural, and product photography. He has the reputation as one of Australia's most sought-after professional photographers who has been producing internationally award-winning images for his clients for over 20 years. He is well known for his innovative images expertly crafted using a blend of both photographic and AI elements.

In preparing this book I interviewed Damien about his experiences using AI image generated images and his views on the impact that it is likely to have on the photographic profession. I have shared extracts from this interview with you here.

I would love to hear your thoughts on AI

I think AI is amazing, it's going to revolutionize industries, not just our industry. I think a lot of people are calling AI, the new internet. What the internet did to the world is what AI will do to our world. It will have a profound effect across all industries, people, or way of life.

I find that exciting because when the internet came in, we didn't know anything about it. So, we couldn't prepare for it. We didn't know what it would do, how it could change our lives, our society. Now that we have an idea about AI being the new thing, we can jump on board, and we can harness the technology, we can embrace it, and we can benefit from it, if you're in early enough. So that's why I said 'Yes, I'm going to adopt it' because I'd like to see what interesting things develop.

I'm also scared by it. And if I don't learn it, I'm going to get forgotten, and my profession will get crushed. And if I stick my head in the sand, like many people are doing, if I don't adapt, clients will not want me, I'm not going to be relevant anymore. And I think that's going to happen really, really, really, quickly. So, for me, I've jumped very much in to learn everything about it that I can.

And it's changing every day, it's almost changing on a minute-by-minute basis. And I talked to a lot of AI experts way beyond my skill level. And they too, are struggling to keep up.

How are you responding to AI in relation to your work?

I'm jumping on board so I can learn as much as I can. I'm still learning.– it's so quickly.

So, for me, I'm not yet at a point where I can offer it as a stand-alone paid service, but I am integrating it into my business. I'm using it as a way to create my own background plates, or elements that I can then cut out or use in my current photography. Blending the two – traditional photography and AI together to create artwork.

What impact do you see AI having on photography?

I have seen that advertising agencies clients of mine are producing artwork and billboard images made completely with AI. Prior to that, they would need a photographer. So, although I'm busy on some aspect of my work, some work has disappeared. There are models, lifestyle images and so on that have been replaced by AI.

So interestingly, it's the high-end work photographic work that's gone. It'll be the middle ground, that will stay, which is the more specific documentary style photography, particular to a client or business. I also think that low-end photography will disappear – this includes product photography and catalog work.

Ecommerce photography is another one that's changing. The whole ecommerce world for photographers is going to fall over very, very quickly. During COVID online businesses went through the roof and this created a lot of work for photographers – producing images for ecommerce, fashion brands, – people had to shop from home, not stores. And they were one of the biggest employers of photographers, nationwide, probably worldwide, because they needed weekly content. That's going to disappear really quickly.

I just had a colleague the other day, who does a lot of ecommerce, which AI has taken over. And she's now gone back to nursing. Just because that market is dying. She can no longer sustain a photography career. I do feel sad, but I have been warning people about what is happening in the industry, but a lot haven't listened.

What is your opinion of the Midjourney program?

Midjourney is the most creative I would say – Midjourney is just wonderful. It's artistic, it's fun, it's creative.

What would you to share with others about the AI revolution?

I don't know what to prepare them for, other than **just to embrace it,** … **get on board and don't fear it.**

Examples of Damien Bredberg's Work

Images created and copyrighted by Damien Bredberg and used here with his permission.

Ayesha Hilton, Digital Artist, Education, Entrepreneur

I met Ayesha online in late 2022 when I was first learning how to use Midjourney. She was offering an online course as an introduction to Midjourney for people who were interested in creating images for card decks.

When Midjourney was first released the only way to access it was through Discord – an online platform popular with video gamers, but not for many of us who found it all rather confusing. Her course was just what I needed to get started, and her passion for Midjourney is contagious – I haven't stopped producing AI art since!

I chose to feature Ayesha's AI art here as I feel it is an example of how image generation can be customized to suit the vibe and look that you are after. Ayesha's images have been carefully crafted with a particular aesthetic in mind – beautiful, ethereal, mystical. She has made a very successful business using her images to set up a stock library, a training and consulting service, and creating both physical and digital products for sale. I have included her responses to my questionnaire as follows.

Please describe the type of work that you do

I love AI and use it daily in my business. I have a range of offerings that have been supported by the use of AI. I design card decks (affirmation, oracle, business, Tarot) and I use AI to help me create images.

I have a course helping others create their own card decks and teach them how to use AI to streamline and speed up the design and marketing process.

I have a stock image membership focused on the spiritual niche where I provide images to members that they can use commercially. I also provide custom deck design and image generation for client projects.

How has AI image generation impacted on you and others in your profession?

AI image generation has totally changed my professional life. I fell in love with Midjourney as soon as I used it. Let's just say, it's the first thing I've been addicted to! There's this beautiful collaboration between myself and Midjourney. It's part prompt craft and part magic. You can enter a well-written prompt and often you get something even more gorgeous than you imagined.

For the card deck creation process, AI image generation has had a huge impact. There has been an increase in the number of decks being created. It has greatly impacted how I personally create decks and how I support my students and clients with their decks. Decks are quicker, easier, and cheaper to create.

Prior to October 2022, my students could source images for their card decks through a stock image website, using their own artwork, or hiring a designer or artist to create the artwork. Many people failed to get the desired result and were really limited in what they could create. There were also the high costs of getting custom images for decks. Many deck creators are using AI-generated images. They are either buying images or generating them personally.

Now, when I look at card decks on platforms like Etsy and Amazon, there are more decks than ever and many now have AI generated images. There are some deck lovers who refuse to buy any decks created with AI. They want to support traditional artists. However, many people are keen on the decks created with AI because of the fantasy effect.

The speed at which a deck can now be made doesn't guarantee quality. I see plenty of terrible decks, where the person hasn't edited out the extra fingers, and you can tell it's made with AI. I like to create decks that don't even look like they are AI generated. That's why I often use painting styles.

Large language models, like ChatGPT and Claude, have also changed how people can create written content for their decks. They can use ChatGPT, for example, to help them research and come up with a theme for their deck, a title and subtitle, and a product description. Then, they can use ChatGPT to help write the messages for their cards or write them themselves and then have their grammar checked by say Grammarly.

Please describe your thoughts, feelings, and beliefs about AI

I love AI! I warn people that once they go down the Midjourney rabbit hole, they are in danger of becoming addicted.

I have a background in web design and I have been an early adopter of technology during my career. When I first got access to Midjourney and ChatGPT in the same month, I was so excited. Some nights, I could barely sleep because I had so many ideas running through my head and I would have to get up, grab my phone and test out prompts. I have generated more than 60,000 images and have no intention of stopping.

There are definitely ethical concerns regarding the use of data to train image models and large language models. We need to be using AI ethically and with consideration of broader societal issues. We also need to have clearer rules regarding copyright and ownership of the images generated. There is much confusion about these sorts of issues.

Please describe how you use AI images in your work

I use AI images in a variety of ways in my work. As a designer, I use the images in my card decks, journals, books, websites, social media, and more. I also generate and distribute images in my stock image membership. When I am designing something, I now choose to generate an image, if possible, rather than purchasing it from a stock image site. It has given me the freedom to create original images to suit specific needs in my business.

Which AI image generation program do you use to create your images?

I love Midjourney. Even though I have used many other programs like DALL-E and Leonardo AI, I still prefer to use Midjourney for most of my images. I have found that Midjourney gives really great artistic style images, which are the ones I prefer. There's more magic in Midjourney images. I think there are some benefits to using DALL-E because images are generated in conversation and can be easily iterated and refined using normal language. However, at the moment, there isn't as much control over different parameters as Midjourney, especially if using DALL-E inside ChatGPT.

Do you have any advice or suggestions for people who might be just starting out with Midjourney or AI art in general?

Approach image generation with a growth mindset. Get excited, play, test prompts. Lean into the magic. And watch out, you might just become addicted. With regard to prompting, I like to start off with a simple prompt and then add to it. I think of it as layering prompts. It's a bit like painting. Start off simple, add more layers, and be careful not to overdo it. I see way too many long prompts that are very ineffective. Start simple, add, test, remove if needed.

While making realistic stock images is doable with Midjourney, I really love to create things that are magical. Sprinkle in some magic with your prompts by using words like magical, fantasy, sparkles, and ethereal, along with painting styles.

What editing do you do on the AI images to turn them into works of art?

I like it most when I have no editing to do. Earlier versions of Midjourney produced too many fingers and if you were doing animals, you often got extra legs. This is less common in the later versions of Midjourney. I edit images in **Photoshop**. I sometimes extend backgrounds, fix up hair (there is often too much hair on the face for my liking), and adjust brightness.

I upscale images for printing with Topaz **Gigapixel**. I also use **Insight Face** with Midjourney on Discord to swap faces with images I have generated (for example, I can put my face onto a painting I have generated). This technology is evolving quickly, and you can now create a "model" of yourself to use for consistent characters with **Art Flow AI**.

I offer a range of courses and services, including the Card Deck Creators Toolkit, Midjourney Magic Course, and Soul Stock Boutique

Email	ayeshahilton@gmail.com
Website	www.ayeshahilton.academy
Instagram	www.instagram.com/ayesha_hilton/
Facebook	www.facebook.com/ayeshahiltonpage
TikTok	www.tiktok.com/@ayeshahiltonofficial
LinkedIn	www.linkedin.com/in/ayeshahilton/

Do you have any other comments, insights, or suggestions?

AI images are everywhere now. When I scroll social media, you can see so many people posting images that are clearly created using AI. I think very soon, we won't be able to distinguish between AI generated images and other images like real photos and paintings. The same is true for video. This will mean even greater impact on jobs.

Examples of Ayesha's AI Work

Images created and copyrighted by Ayesha Hilton and used here with her permission.

Dirk Fleischmann: Photographer, Digital, and AI Artist

I first came across the artwork of Dirk Fleischmann (known online as **Niphisi**) on Instagram where I was attracted to his intriguing minimalist images. I wasn't the only one entranced by his simple, but very evocative images, he has over 158,000 followers on Instagram, and another 34,000 on Facebook. I contacted him through his website to find out more about his artwork and he graciously allowed me to profile him and his work here.

Dirk's work represents a very skillful merging of the mediums of photography, digital art, and AI to create unique works of art which are very popular worldwide among the art community. He is a wonderful example of someone who has embraced the creative opportunities offered by AI art and integrated them with his existing skills to create truly unique artwork. If you are looking for inspiration for how AI image generation can be utilized as part of a broader art practice, check out his work using the links provided at the end of this section.

Name: Dirk Fleischmann (known as Niphisi online)

How do you create your unique works of art?

My works of art are created through a blend of different styles of graphic art. Original creations with realistic photography are combined with AI elements and distorted using iPhone apps. By adjusting colors and cutting out individual elements, a minimalist overall image is created in the form of a new composition.

Hardly any of the images generated by AI exactly match my vision. I therefore add additional elements through various editing techniques. It is usually a long journey from the proposed AI image to the completion of the final artwork.

Where do you show and sell your AI artwork?

I mainly showcase my artworks on my website www.niphisi.com. There, I present various versions of my works such as prints, calendars, canvases, postcards, and custom-made pieces. The initial contact is made through an inquiry form, which is more personal and allows me to address requests and questions. It's important to me to connect with potential buyers, not only to offer an online shop.

In addition, I share my work on social media platforms like Instagram (www.instagram.com/niphisi/) and Facebook (www.facebook.com/niphisi) My work is also represented in several exhibitions.

Do you feel there is a market for AI generated artwork?

Yes, definitely. In my opinion, a picture doesn't always have to depict reality. It should visually appeal to the viewer, evoke their emotions and feelings, and create an atmosphere of calm and serenity. A harmonious interplay of colors between the elements is also important. It is important to me to take my viewers and followers into my own world, which is also reflected in the positive feedback on social media.

I do get criticism of my work however – this includes comments from traditional photographers who completely reject the use of AI. This results in me having to deal with hate comments on social media. I believe every era has its own art form. Currently, the use of AI is prevalent in all areas of life. Resisting often leads to frustration, while combining different techniques may be motivating.

Do you use any other programs apart from Midjourney to create your artwork?

In general, I edit my work on the iPhone using the following apps: Canva, Picsart, Photoroom.

Do you have any suggestions for someone just starting out with AI art?

Use your own imagination and creativity when creating images with AI. Give it a try.

If you would like to see more of Dirk's work I have provided a few links below:

Instagram: www.instagram.com/niphisi/
Facebook: www.facebook.com/niphisi
Website: https://niphisi.com/
Email: dirk_fleischmann67@web.de
Artpeople Gallery (2024, January 10) https://artpeoplegallery.com/niphisi-show-minimalism-in-its-beautiful-purest-form).
Get Inspired Magazine: His work is featured on the cover of Issue 62 https://getinspiredmagazine.com/

Examples of Dirk Fleischmann's (Niphisi) Work

Images created and copyrighted by Dirk Fleischmann and used with his permission.

Using Midjourney for Personal Enjoyment

There are many millions of users of Midjourney who are using it for their own enjoyment and as a creative outlet. Since the release of image generating programs there has been an explosion in the social media sites providing Midjourney users with a forum to share their creations. I have listed a few examples of very active AI Facebook groups below:

- Midjourney Official (653,000 members)
- Midjourney Prompt Tricks (246,000 members)
- AI revolution (205,000 members)
- Midjourney Unofficial (177,000 members)
- Midjourney Images and Insights (26,000 members)
- Midjourney AI/Digital Art (21,000 members)

On Instagram there are millions of images using hashtags containing the word Midjourney:

- • #midjourney: 7,083,921 posts,
- • #midjourneyart: 3,502,383 posts,
- • #midjourneyai: 2,173,068 posts,
- • #midjourneyartwork: 1,264,104 posts.

The majority of these social media sites feature images created by people who use Midjourney just for fun. In a recent study, 83% of users reported using Midjourney as a form of art therapy and mood enhancer – "it makes you feel better, destress and forget about time for a while, that benefits the body and the mind" (Krivec, 2023).

Judging by its incredible popularity on social media platforms, a lot of people get a great sense of enjoyment from creating and sharing images online. Image generation is also increasingly being used as an art therapy tool for people with disabilities, mental health challenges, and in stress reduction programs. It allows people without any formal training in art, or who have physical limitations preventing them using traditional art mediums, to explore their creativity and the many benefits this can bring.

To better understand the popularity of AI generated art for personal, rather than professional uses, I interviewed a passionate user of Midjourney who is an administrator for a very popular Facebook group: **Midjourney Images and Insights.** which you can access at www.facebook.com/groups/ourbestm idjourneyimages. This public group currently has over 26,000 members.

Pseudonym: Jade Jenerai
Contact details: Email: jadejenerai@gmail.com

Please describe how you discovered AI

My initial exposure to AI art was through YouTube, where I became fascinated by the concept of generating art simply using a keyboard. This intrigue led me to delve deeper into the realm of AI art by watching more videos specific to the AI tool of interest.

Which AI image generation program/s do you use to create your images?

Upon viewing the diverse range of images produced by various AI tools such as Stable Diffusion, Nightcafe, Leonardo AI, and Midjourney, I consistently found myself drawn to those generated by Midjourney. However, it took me several months to commit to purchasing an annual Midjourney subscription. Initially, I began with Stable Diffusion as it was free, but ultimately made the decision to transition to Midjourney.

Please describe your thoughts, feelings, and beliefs about AI

My motto "Embrace change, for with change comes opportunity" holds true for my thoughts on AI.

Do you use AI-generated art as part of your work, or just for your enjoyment?

AI Art is a hobby for me.

If you generate AI art for enjoyment, could you please describe what you like about it

Thanks to AI text-to-image software, anyone can tap into their inner artist. The ability to swiftly generate diverse images enables me to explore many ideas, styles, and subjects in just a day. Initially, I created a Facebook page and began sharing my creations as a personal challenge to learn Midjourney, but I've come to relish the interactions with those who appreciate my work. Moreover, engaging with fellow creators and absorbing their knowledge has proven invaluable in my journey.

Do you do any additional editing of your AI?

Midjourney output is fantastic, but being a long-time Photoshop user, I inevitably find myself compelled to fine-tune my Midjourney images.

You have been very active online helping people keep up to date with changes in Midjourney and suggesting prompts for them to try. I would love to hear more about these activities

I've been using Midjourney for about a year now, starting from Midjourney Version 5. One pivotal point in my growth was becoming a Facebook administrator for a group founded by my mentor and AI Artist, Irina Shamaeva (aka The Prompter). Together with three other administrators, we uphold the group's ethos of sharing prompts and other valuable information in our community.

www.facebook.com/groups/ourbestmidjourneyimages

Beyond this group, I actively engage in several other Facebook AI Image communities. Being part of diverse communities fuels my continuous learning.

Attending the weekly Midjourney Office Hours meetings has been another enriching experience for me. Led by the Midjourney CEO, David Holtz, these sessions offer insights into upcoming features and provide a glimpse into the company's culture, which I find fascinating.

Regularly delving into the Midjourney Discord channels has also proven fruitful. The announcements and FAQs are a treasure trove of information. Recently, I've begun attending the weekly Promptcraft Live events, which have further expanded my knowledge and skills.

These experiences collectively contribute to my growth as an AI artist, and I enjoy sharing my knowledge with others.

Do you have any advice or suggestions for people who might be just starting out with Midjourney or AI art in general? Please feel free to add any other comments

Everyone undergoes an awkward phase at the beginning, where images may not meet expectations – it's all part of the learning curve. Push through and you will be rewarded.

Make the most of Midjourney's resources available on its Discord server, such as live events, community support, etc. Dive into the Midjourney documentation! You can find official documentation online, as well as detailed FAQs regularly updated on the Midjourney Discord channel. Attend the weekly Promptcraft Live events – they're incredibly beneficial, especially for newcomers. Check the Midjourney Discord server for dates and times.

Follow me on Facebook or Instagram, where I share prompts for my images, along with valuable information and updates about Midjourney:

www.facebook.com/jadejenerai/, www.instagram.com/jadejenerai/

Explore the Resources List on my Facebook page, including vloggers I follow regularly, along with supplementary tools and websites for Midjourney users. Engage with AI artist communities on your preferred social networks.

Experiment, experiment, experiment! Start with simpler prompts rather than diving into lengthy ones when beginning your journey. Take part in ongoing challenges offered by various communities. My Facebook group provides daily challenges, and several other groups also organize similar activities.

Be generous in sharing your knowledge, and good karma shall follow!

Examples of Jade Jenerai's Work

Images created by Jade Jenerai presented here are used with her permission.

Using Midjourney Images to Raise Awareness of Social Issues

Throughout the book I have illustrated some of the many and varied ways that AI imagery can be used across different discipline areas. In this section I feature the work of an Okki Peach Kim, an AI artist who has chosen to use her artwork to raise awareness of social issues that are important to her. Her words and images are presented here with her permission.

The creativity, flexibility and adaptability of AI image generation makes it an ideal tool to produce images that catch people's attention and help communicate their message.

Animal Conservation

I was scrolling through Facebook recently and came across a post by Okki Peace Kim, a Korean AI designer and artist, who is encouraging viewers to consider how they can use their AI art ethically for good causes.

> With the proliferation and rapid development of AI image generators, we're often drowning in a sea of meaningless images. But the good thing about generative AI is that you can create educational materials for children or campaign images for the environment without caging or training animals. We can create posters with beautiful floral arrangements without cutting down trees or picking flowers. Also, wouldn't it reduce the environmental pollution caused by using transportation for filming?
>
> *Okki Peace Kim: Facebook post Mar 31, 2024 www.facebook.com/okkpd*

Okki uses her artwork to raise awareness and funds for animal conservation projects by selling the prompt that she used to generate these Endangered Animals. All images and descriptions shown here by Okki Peace Kim are used with her permission.

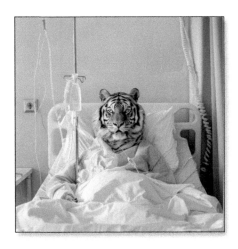

Image created by Okki Peace Kim
Source: www.facebook.com/okkpd
March 28, 2024

"The Last King of a Forgotten Realm: Lying in a hospital bed, this tiger was once the sovereign of nature. Now he needs our help. If we do not act now, these majestic creatures may soon exist only in photographs. Let's protect their habitat and our collective future".

Image created by Okki Peace Kim
Source: www.instagram.com/p/C5CpSYvxL-o/

"The silent struggle of recovery. These polar bear's eyes have a story to tell. A story about his critically endangered colleagues. We can change their story with small daily choices. Please put it into action now".

If you are interested in buying her prompt or supporting her conservation efforts, go to PromptBase.com and search for Animal Anthropomorphism Photo Hospitals by @ethicalprompt.

According to Okki's Instagram post, the images are part of her UTOPIA2524 series in which she imagines:

> a future where animals are the masters of the planet … It's a different direction than many creators envision for the future, where robots and technology rule the world … . While AI image generators are often viewed negatively, they can also allow us to do work that is a force for good. AI-generated images have given people the freedom to express themselves, but the more we do so, the more we need to take time to reflect on the important things in life that are easy to miss.

> With AI image generators, you can create images that are as colorful and unrealistic as you want. But with a little more thought, we can also do good with the benefits we gain by taking a positive approach to the environment.

ethical_prompt:: www.instagram.com/p/C5zmCxAR-uR/?img_index=1

Okki takes a very ethical approach to her AI image generation and encourages all image creators to do the same. Her social media name is @ethical_prompt and, as she indicates on her site:

- "I don't use other people's creations as a prompt.
- I don't use names or images of actual characters.
- I don't use a prompt with the artist's name on it (excluding artists and landscapes in history whose copyright has expired).
- I don't produce material that causes historical, political, or social disruption".

In addition to her Endangered Animals series shown above, she has some other amazing AI artwork on her Instagram site, often accompanied by inspirational text. I have included a few examples from her "We are born from the same flower":

Image by Okki Peace Kim Source: www.instagram.com/p/C5sex66PdJI

"Humans and nature have a deep-rooted connection, it's our nature and the source of our existence.

Close your eyes and imagine yourself relaxing in the arms of nature. We are part of nature, and our souls heal and grow when we feel in the moment".

Image by Okki Peace Kim Source: www.instagram. com/p/C5prbtbxhz-

"The rare white tiger reminds us of the preciousness and vulnerability of nature in the human world. Our mother earth is represented by the bud of the kala lily."

"We grow from the same flower, from the same mother's womb. The home we share with nature, Earth, is a beautiful place that is sacred and should be protected".

Her work is beautifully displayed using AI-created elegant room mock-ups.

Image created by Okki Peace Kim (ethical_prompt)
www.instagram.com/p/C5zmCxAR-uR/?img_index=3

UTOPIA2524 We Are Born from the Same Flower series
digital mockup display.

Another thought-provoking series featured on her Instagram site is the "Plastic Runway" series. This series is a fashion show that imagines a time when the only resource left on Earth is a non-biodegradable plastic:

Image created by Okki Peace Kim (ethical_prompt)
www.instagram.com/p/C16FHv1vBHq/?img_index=1

Mental Health

Okki's work is not just limited to raising awareness of conservation and environmental causes. Another series of her artwork focuses on the issue of mental health:

> I realized as an adult that I had difficulty expressing my emotions, and I wanted to express through my work the realization that 'humans are beautiful for feeling sadness'.

Her "The flying fish series – Lalamikikko's Wonderland" is an example of work on this theme:

"This work is related to the panic disorder I am experiencing. I often feel stuffy breathing like a fish out of the water. I used to get better when I took a break imagining flying fish" … I drew a big fish and a pretty girl that I met in my dream. This work was based on my sketch.

@ethical_prompt www.instagram.com/ethical_prompt

Image created by Okki Peace Kim (ethical_prompt)
Source: www.instagram.com/p/CxcBjgxvAOx/?img_index=1

Image created by Okki Peace Kim (ethical_prompt)
Source:
www.instagram.com/p/Cx-Id_irWuU/?img_index=1

Okki is a very talented artist who has embraced AI generated images as an important tool in expressing her creativity. Check out more of Okki Peace Kim's work:

Facebook: www.facebook.com/okkpd
Instagram: www.instagram.com/ethical_prompt/
YouTube: www.youtube.com/@ethical_prompt
Website: www.utopia2524.com

Making Money with Midjourney

One of the questions that pops up quite often on the various Midjourney Facebook groups that I follow is whether there is a way to make money from images created using Midjourney. The answer is definitely *Yes*, and earlier in this chapter, I presented the work of number of creatives that are doing just that.

While many people using Midjourney do so as part of their employment, there are also other more entrepreneurial applications of AI art. A recent article that appeared in the Worklife magazine (Worklife Editorial, 2023) reviewed various ways that AI is being used in animation, graphic design, architecture, interior, and furniture design. The article goes on to provide a number of suggestions for business applications where you could make use of your AI skills:

- **Personalized Artwork:** Create customized or personalized artwork for clients.
- **Art Consulting:** Make use of AI tools to assist clients to choose art pieces for their homes or offices.
- **Stock Photos:** Generate images for use on stock photography websites or create your own stock library.
- **Templates:** Midjourney can be used to create templates for logos, branding, social media graphics, and other marketing materials which can be tweaked to fit their specific needs.
- **Digital Art Prints:** Create high-quality digital art prints, canvases, and other products to be sold online on marketplaces such as Etsy or on your own e-commerce shop (Worklife Editorial, 2023).

The other place to look for ideas on how you can monetize your Midjourney images is YouTube. In recent years YouTube has exploded with videos on how to make money using AI images. There are hundreds of people claiming to have made millions of dollars by producing products featuring AI images and selling them through online ecommerce sites such as Etsy or Redbubble.

While I treat these claims with hefty dose of skepticism, you might like to explore the possibilities if you are looking for ways to supplement your income. In the next section I have provided details of two of the people that you might find helpful to follow on YouTube if you are interested in "making millions with Midjourney". Please note this information does not come with a money back guarantee!!

Wholesale Ted

My favorite YouTube "money maker guide" is Sarah Crisp who goes by the name of Wholesale Ted on YouTube. She is a young NZ woman with over 1.2 million followers who posts YouTube videos regularly, many showing how she uses Midjourney images to create a range of products using Print-on-Demand (POD) platforms.

If you are not familiar with POD it is a service that allows you to upload your images, which are then printed on a wide range of products, including T-shirts, hoodies, mugs, phone cases, cushions, and more. Customers can choose from a variety of designs, colors, and sizes online, and the product is produced and shipped directly to the customer. POD platforms such as Red Bubble, Gelato, Printify, and Printful enable designers and entrepreneurs to create custom products without investing in large quantities upfront.

One of the Wholesale Ted videos you might like to watch to get an idea of ways to "monetize" your AI art is: "5 AI Side Hustles that actually make money" (www.youtube.com/watch?v=1ZP6sXWBqGk). In this video, Sarah demonstrates how she uses Midjourney images to:

- Create products such as pillows and shower curtains with Midjourney images using Print on Demand. These products can be sold on sites such as Etsy, RedBubble, or your own ecommerce website.
- Sell prompts on PromptBase and Etsy. Some of the best-selling prompt packs are for coloring books, images to print on T-shirts, and product mockups.

If you would like more information on how to use POD to sell products with your images go to Wholesale Ted's YouTube channel and click on the blue link wholesaleted.com/4-step. Here you can provide your email address to receive a free eBook where she outlines the process.

On the Wholesale Ted channel Sarah lists many other videos that you might find helpful, giving you step-by-step guides to choosing and setting up a POD account, and creating a Shopify website or an Etsy store to sell your products.

For a more detailed training course on how to launch an ecommerce business to monetize your images Wholesale Ted has set up a subscription-based platform "The Ecomm Clubhouse" which has lots of useful training videos and written guides to help you through the process. I found this course helpful – it is much more detailed and easier to navigate than watching random YouTube videos.

Alek Sheffield

The other YouTube channel that I have found useful when learning about making money from AI art is that of Alek Sheffield – his YouTube name is "Alek". You can find Alek's videos on YouTube at www.yout ube.com/@aleksheffy where he has over 430,000 subscribers and his individual videos regularly hit over 1 million views.

Alek's approach to making money is to carefully research what is trending on sites such as Etsy and to produce similar material using Midjourney. His techniques do require a pretty good grasp of Midjourney and its various commands. However, you will find all the skills you need covered in Chapters 5 and 6 of this book.

One video of Alek's that you might like to watch is "The best AI passive income side hustle 2024" (www. youtube.com/watch?v=BD9aVGh-vmc). In this video, he approaches AI image generation from a business, rather than artistic, perspective. His business model emphasizes the need to spend time researching trends to see what customers are buying.

Alek researches the digital download art that is selling well on Etsy and uses this "rustic, moody, vintage style" to write a prompt in Midjourney. The video was made in January 2024 so he uses the Discord version of Midjourney – you can just ignore these instructions and use the online version of the program which is covered in this book instead (it is much easier!).

Alek takes you through the process of creating the image and preparing it for sale by using different aspect ratios to suit the customer's needs. As the files are too large to load directly onto the Etsy site, he explains that he saves them in a folder on Google Drive or Dropbox. He then creates a cover letter with a link to the online folder for the customer to download. This letter is converted to PDF and uploaded to Etsy as a digital download.

In the final section of the video Alek describes how to sell these images as products on the POD platform Printify. This can be integrated into an Etsy store allowing your customer to purchase your image and have it printed and sent directly to them. Printify has a free version for you to try, or you can use the affiliate link that Alek provides on his YouTube channel to get two months free Premium membership. This gives you a 20% discount on the cost of each of the products.

If you are strongly motivated to make money using your AI art you might like to check out Alek's other videos on his YouTube channel where he explains how he creates phone cases, mugs, T-shirts, and many other print-on-demand products. While you may not make the millions of dollars that he has apparently made, he certainly has some ideas that you might like to try out.

Selling Prompts

Another way to make money with Midjourney is to sell your successful prompts on a site like PromptBase (https://promptbase.com/). PromptBase is a marketplace, which sells prompts suitable for use in programs such as Midjourney, DALL-E, and Stable Diffusion. Sellers get to keep 80% of each sale, while PromptBase takes a 20% fee that covers website and administration costs.

If you are interested in selling your prompts I have included a few tips for you below:

Quality matters: To attract buyers, your prompts should be well-crafted, specific, and effective in generating high-quality responses from AI models like Midjourney. Identify the types of users who would benefit from your prompts (e.g., artists, writers, designers) and tailor your prompts to their needs.

Write clear and concise descriptions: Provide detailed information about what your prompt does, what kind of output to expect, and any specific instructions or tips for use. Use relevant categories and tags to make your prompts easily discoverable by users searching for specific types of content. Ensure you comply with PromptBase's terms of service, content policies, and any specific requirements for sellers.

Set competitive pricing: Research similar prompts on PromptBase to determine fair and competitive pricing for your prompts.

Utilize marketing and promotion: Share your prompts on social media, forums, and other platforms to attract potential buyers and drive sales.

Keep your prompts up-to-date: Regularly update and refine your prompts to reflect changes in AI models and user needs, maintaining their effectiveness and relevance.

Engage with the community: Interact with potential buyers, respond to feedback, and contribute to the PromptBase community to build your reputation and promote your prompts. Track your sales, user feedback, and ratings to refine your prompts and marketing strategies, improving your overall success on PromptBase.

Before choosing which prompts to sell you might want to check out the best-selling Midjourney prompts showing on the PromptBase site. The site lists the most popular Midjourney prompts of all time, and the most popular for the last month.

References

Krivec, R. (2023, September 14). Midjourney statistics (how many people use Midjourney?). *Colorlib.* https://colorlib.com/wp/midjourney-statistics/#h-how-many-people-use-midjourney

Worklife Editorial. (2023, 22 February). These artists are using AI as a creative partner – see how! *Worklife Blog.* www.worklife.vc/blog/ai-artist

8

Additional Resources

Introduction

The AI image generation world is changing at an amazing pace so to keep up you will need to continue learning new skills and adapting to new developments. Each of the image generating programs, including Midjourney, are updated regularly with new features and improvements made to the image generation process. Over the past two years the improvement in the images has been staggering, with more to come!

In this final chapter, I provide a range of resources that you might find useful as you continue to develop your Midjourney skills and find ways to utilize the images you create.

Official Midjourney Documentation

The Midjourney program has official documentation that provides details about the program and the commands available. To access this resource, click on the **Help** button on the bottom left of the screen, and go to the **Resources section**.

DOI: 10.1201/9781003541677-8

This link will take you to the Midjourney website: https://docs.midjourney.com/

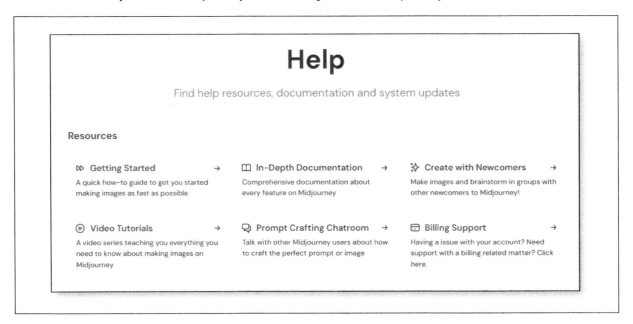

Click on the link to the **Getting Started**. In the guide click on the heading of interest to view details of the how to use the various commands.

It is a good idea to check this site regularly to keep up to date with changes in the Midjourney program. This book was written in June 2024, showing the features and layout available at that time. Given how quickly Midjourney updates, what you see on your own screen may differ from that shown in the book. You may also find that Midjourney changes the name of a tool, or the way in which it can be accessed. The Midjourney documentation will be a useful resource for you to resolve any issues you might have.

> If you notice that any of your screens look different to what is shown in the book you can keep up to date with changes to the Midjourney program on my website. You will also find videos showing how you can make the most out of Midjourney.
> You can access the website using the link: https://linktr.ee/juliepallant

Midjourney News

One of the things I love about using Midjourney is that it is easy to keep up to date with changes, and to hear what the developers are working on. They regularly release announcements about recent changes and welcome feedback to improve the program. They have office hours each week on the Discord platform to discuss changes, planned developments, and to allow users to ask questions.

To check out the recent updates to Midjourney, click on the **Updates** button located on the left-hand side of the Midjourney screen. The changes are listed in chronological order with the most recent at the top.

YouTube

The other resource to keep you up to date with developments in Midjourney and to expand your skills, is YouTube. There are numerous videos on YouTube that review new features released and show how to use Midjourney more effectively. It is just a case of finding a presenter that suits your style – I find some try too hard to be sensational and are very annoying!

Warning: Keep an eye out for the more recent YouTube tutorials that show how to use the online Midjourney platform. Most of the videos created prior to May 2024 feature the previous Discord version of the Midjourney program, which still works, but is more difficult to set up.

Two of the people that I like to follow on YouTube are Woolyfern and Future Tech Pilot.

- **Woolyfern** posts regularly on YouTube with updates on the Midjourney program. You can find her at www.youtube.com/@woollyferncreative and she also has a website/blog at https://woollyferncreat ive.com/. Included are some very detailed posts about various features of Midjourney.
- **Future Tech Pilot** (real name Nolan Michaels) has a YouTube site with over 47,000 subscribers. If you click on the Midjourney Tutorial blue link on his site, you can see a list of 95 videos covering many of the features of Midjourney. Focus on the most recent videos that refer to the online version of Midjourney.

Facebook and Instagram

You might find it helpful to join one or more of the many Facebook sites where Midjourney users share images, and the prompts used to generate them. There is an incredible variety of AI images that are posted to these sites. While not all may be to your liking, there could be things to be learnt from the prompts that are shared. There are often people in these groups that you can turn to for help if you have a problem with creating prompts.

Some sites I have found useful are:

- Midjourney Official (653,000 members)
- Midjourney Prompt Tricks (246,000 members)
- AI revolution (205,000 members)
- Midjourney Unofficial (177,000 members)
- Midjourney Images and Insights (26,000 members)
- Midjourney AI/Digital Art (21,000 members)

Instagram can also be a great source of inspiration – I have listed some of the commonly used Midjourney hashtags below:

- #midjourney (7,083,921 posts)
- #midjourneyart (3,502,383 posts)
- #midjourneyai (2,173,068 posts)
- #midjourneyartwork (1,264,104 posts)

You might find it fun to post some of the Midjourney images you have created and get feedback from the group. People on the AI sites are generally friendly. If you post to more general (non-AI) sites, you can sometimes get negative reactions from people who are anti-AI.

If you are posting online, I encourage you to make it clear that the image was created using AI – I also specify that I used the Midjourney program. Ethically, this means people are not being fooled into thinking it is a "real" photo.

Additional Software

While AI-generated images can be strikingly unique and creative, they may lack the finesse and precision of traditional digital artworks or photographs. To get the best from your Midjourney images, it is often helpful to apply some additional editing to ensure that they are as high a quality as possible, and suitable for the intended purpose.

There are a number of additional pieces of software that you might find useful if you intend to use your images commercially. If you are using AI purely for your own pleasure or sharing on social media, please don't feel any pressure to apply the editing suggested below.

Software to Catalog and Organize Your Images

When I first started using Midjourney I was rather obsessed (still am!) and I produced a lot of images in a short period of time. I was faced with the challenge of organizing and storing these images so that I could retrieve the images that I wanted in the future.

As a photographer, I use Adobe Lightroom Classic to import and catalog my photographic images into folders and collections. This program also proved to be a valuable tool for organizing my library of Midjourney images, which is now well over 15,000 images.

If you are not familiar with Adobe Lightroom Classic it is a very powerful program that allows you to import images, set up a folder structure, rename files, and add keywords. It also incorporates an image editing module that provides a whole suite of tools for you to modify your images, including crop and change the aspect ratio; adjust the exposure, contrast, and color of the whole image or selected areas; remove minor distractions; and add a vignette.

If you are using Midjourney to generate images for your work, commercial clients, or to sell online you will need to plan how you will store and organize your images. You might want to consider subscribing to an Adobe Creative Cloud package that includes both Lightroom Classic and Photoshop (this program is discussed in depth in the next section). There are a variety of packages available. Check out the Photography package which includes access to both Lightroom Classic and Photoshop – two really great tools that will help you make the most of your Midjourney images.

Photo Editing Software

When you generate images in Midjourney you may get extra arms or hands, unwanted elements, or colors that you don't like. If you are selling your images, or creating them for clients, it is important that you develop the skills to edit your images to ensure they are free from these defects.

One of the best all-round tools for making changes to the content of your images I have found is Adobe Photoshop. Photoshop is available as part of the Photography package on Adobe.com, along with Lightroom

Classic (discussed in the previous section). Lightroom Classic allows you to organize and catalog your images and perform basic edits, while Photoshop gives you the tools to make changes to the pixels in the image, for example, to remove an unwanted arm or extra fingers.

For a free alternative program, with some of the functionality of Photoshop, you might want to check out Photopea (www.Photopea.com).

Although Photoshop is a complex and sometimes overwhelming program, it is definitely worth learning if you are a professional and selling your images. Each of the artists and photographers that I highlighted in Chapter 7 indicated that their images had undergone considerable editing to achieve the final result.

I have listed below some of the ways that Photoshop can be used to improve your images:

Adjustments to exposure and color: Colors in AI-generated images can appear over saturated or unnatural. Photoshop offers comprehensive color correction tools such as Curves and Color Balance that can adjust tones, color, temperature, and saturation in an image. The Camera Raw Filter also provides a whole range of tools that allow you to conduct preliminary edits to the exposure and contrast to bring out the best in your image.

Retouching imperfections: AI-generated images can include flaws such as smudges, splashes, lines, or ghosting effects around edges. Photoshop tools, including the Remove Tool, Healing Brush, Clone Stamp, and Patch Tool are useful for cleaning up these areas, making your final image look more professional.

Adding or modifying elements: Sometimes, an AI-generated image might be missing a component, or you might wish to add new elements to enhance the composition (e.g. swapping a background). The use of layers, along with Photoshop's masks, brushes, and other tools, makes it possible to customize the original AI creation to better suit your needs.

When you have a particular requirement for an image, using Photoshop gives you a lot more control than attempting to modify it in Midjourney. This is particularly the case when adding text to an image, something that Midjourney does not yet do reliably.

The recent addition of a Generative Fill option in Photoshop makes the removal and replacement of sections of your image amazingly easy. You can even use the AI image generation capabilities built into Photoshop to create new elements or backgrounds using a text prompt. In my work I have used Generative Fill to replace the backgrounds, clothing, hats, and accessories of images created in Midjourney.

Advanced compositing: For more complex edits, such as combining multiple AI-generated images into a single composition or integrating AI elements with photographic images, Photoshop's layers, masks, and blending modes give you a high level of control. To composite well you will need to invest some time and energy into learning how to use the program effectively to create professional looking images.

Preparing for print or display: Whether your AI-generated artwork is intended for print or digital display, Photoshop's tools for resizing, cropping, and format conversion ensure that the image is suitable for its final medium. This includes adjusting the image size, aspect ratio, resolution, and color profiles, to suit specific purposes (e.g. Instagram post, flyer, document).

To demonstrate how Photoshop can be used as part of the AI image generation workflow I have provided a few examples of my own work where I have utilized various tools in Photoshop. I have briefly outlined the steps that I took to modify each image. The aim is not to teach you Photoshop (that is the topic for another book!), but instead to show you the issues that I addressed, and the steps that I took to achieve the outcome that I wanted. More examples of using Adobe Photoshop to modify Midjourney images are available on my website (https://linktr.ee/juliepallant).

Example 1: Changing the Color of an Image

The image of the polar bear shown below on the left is the original image generated by Midjourney. I didn't like the color – it was too green and too dark. I imported the image into Photoshop and used the White Balance sliders in the Camera Raw Filter to adjust the color of the image. I also increased the exposure of the image.

Original Midjourney Image

Edited in Photoshop to change the color and
to lighten the image

FIGURE 8.1
Original Midjourney image and the revised version edited in Photoshop.

Example 2: Removal of Unwanted Elements

In the example below I used the Content Aware Fill tool in Photoshop to remove unwanted signatures on the bottom right of the image. These are not real signatures of an artist that Midjourney has copied – rather they are fake signatures that Midjourney thinks are needed, given the type of images it has been trained on.

Original Midjourney image

Edited in Photoshop using the Content
Aware Fill tool to remove signatures

FIGURE 8.2
Bird image before and after editing in Photoshop to remove fake signatures.

Example 3: Swapping Headshot Backgrounds

Figure 8.3 Original photograph taken in the studio by the author.

In this example I took a "real" photograph of mine taken of a client in the studio (shown in Figure 8.3) and swapped the plain background with a number of different backgrounds created in Midjourney.

©Julie Pallant

Figure 8.4 Subject cut out and placed on her own layer.

In the photograph of the client file, I used the **Select Subject** tool to select her and pressed **Ctrl J** to put her on her own layer with a transparent background which shows as a checkerboard pattern) (see Figure 8.4).

©Julie Pallant

Figure 8.5 Subject with new Midjourney background.

I copied the extracted client layer across to the office background image and used the **Transform** tool to resize and position her in the scene.

©Julie Pallant

To ensure that both the client and background layers match in terms of brightness and color I used the **Harmonization** option under the **Neural Filter** menu. This provides a quick, easy, and effective way of matching the newly imported material with the background.

With the subject extracted and on her own layer, it is easy to experiment with positioning her on different backgrounds. In the example below I created three different backgrounds in Midjourney, and I used the **Harmonization Neural Filter** each time to adjust her coloring to suit each of the backgrounds.

FIGURE 8.6

Examples of the subject composited with different Midjourney backgrounds.
©Julie Pallant

As a photographer I find this an effective way to offer the client a range of different looks from the one image. You can generate many different backgrounds to suit the client's needs (formal/informal, indoors/ outdoors, corporate backdrops, specific locations).

One thing you need to consider when swapping backgrounds is to match the lighting of the subject and the background image. Consider the direction of the light and whether it is harsh or soft. Check the direction of the shadows, and how quickly the light drops off.

You can include information about the light in the prompt used to create the background in Midjourney. For example: you could ask for: backlit with golden afternoon light; light coming from the side casting long shadows; harsh, direct, strong contrast light; or soft, even light.

The other issues that can impact on the success of a composite are the camera position and angle, and the depth of field evident in each component. Both the background, and the person or object, will need to look as if they have been shot from the same angle (eye height, above, below) and with a similar depth of field (shallow or deep). You can specify this information in your Midjourney prompt. If necessary, there are tools in Photoshop that allow you to blur the background, for example, to match a portrait taken close-up with a low aperture value.

When planning an image where you are compositing a person into a Midjourney background you could photograph the person first, and then write a prompt to create an AI background to suit the lighting, camera angle and depth of field used in the photograph. Alternatively, you may choose to design a set of backgrounds first and then plan your shoot of the person to match the requirements of the background.

I demonstrate this second approach in the example below.

Example 4: Creating Templates

Creating background templates in Midjourney to use across multiple clients is an effective way for studio-based photographers to boost their income. For portraits, instead of shooting a client on location, you can shoot in the controlled environment of the studio and then use Photoshop to paste the image of the client into a background of their choosing. The same approach can be taken to product photography – prepare a background in Midjourney and composite a photograph of the product into the image.

While you can purchase digital backgrounds from sites like Etsy, a more flexible and cheaper option is to make your own in Midjourney. Depending on your area of interest, you can ask Midjourney to create backgrounds suitable for sport portraits, headshots, family portraiture, fantasy portraits, glamour shoots, Christmas themed shoots, product photography, food photography. I have included a few examples in Figure 8.7.

FIGURE 8.7
Examples of backgrounds created using Midjourney.

If you generate a Midjourney background but would like it to be more blurred, you can use the Gaussian Blur filter available under the Filter menu in Photoshop. This tool is also useful for smoothing out any unwanted texture or uneven color in an image.

Example 5: Creating a Greeting Card

Midjourney images can be used in a wide variety of ways, for both professional applications and more personal purposes. In the next example I explain how I used Midjourney to create a customized greeting card for a friend who wanted a quirky, one-of-a-kind wedding card for her niece who was getting married. The whole family are mad keen cat lovers, so she wanted the card to feature cats.

I generated the original image in Midjourney (shown on the left below) and used a number of tools in Photoshop (PS) to create the final card shown on the right.

Original Midjourney image

After editing in Photoshop to extend background, add rectangles and text

FIGURE 8.8

Editing a Midjourney image in Photoshop to create a greeting card.

I have outlined my editing process here:

- Resized the Midjourney image to create a square aspect ratio and extended the background using the **Generative Expand** tool in Photoshop. This also created new material for the female cat's dress that was missing in the original image. Extra space was created above the couple to add a text box.
- Created a duplicate of the background on the left-hand side, flipped it horizontally and then used it to replace the background on the right-hand side of the image. This removed distracting elements present on the right-hand side and helped to create a more symmetrical composition.
- Used a **Curves** adjustment layer to darken the background to create a vignette around the couple. This helped them to pop forward in the image.
- Created semi-transparent rectangles to provide a background for the text.
- Added three text layers for the names of the couple and the top "Con-cat-ulations".
- Used **Topaz Gigapixel AI** to enlarge and sharpen the details of the image for printing onto a card.
- Adjusted the color profile for printing. Created and exported the image as both low-resolution (for social media) and high-resolution (for printing) JPG files.

Example 6: Turning Photos into Paintings

Swapping backgrounds is a great way to rescue images that might otherwise end up in the recycle bin. The image below of a macaw that I took on a trip to the zoo with my grandson was one such image. The poor bird was being carried around the zoo on the hand of a keeper – not exactly the wildlife image that I had in mind. I swapped the uninspiring background for an abstract image I generated in Midjourney that matched the color of the bird.

On the left is the original photo, in the middle, is the Midjourney background I generated, and on the right is the final composited image. I print my composited bird images onto large canvases, and they have sold well in a number of galleries and markets in my local area.

Original photograph of a macaw taken at a zoo

Abstract background generated in Midjourney

Final image created by merging the photograph and Midjourney image in Photoshop

© Julie Pallant

FIGURE 8.9
Combining my photograph of a macaw with a Midjourney background.
©Julie Pallant

I have summarized the steps used in Photoshop to achieve the final result.

- Imported the original bird photo into Photoshop and made adjustments to the exposure and contrast using a **Curves** adjustment layer.
- Created an image of a dead branch in Midjourney and imported this as a layer in Photoshop.
- Replaced the keeper's hand with the dead branch by adjusting the branch using the **Transform** tool and applying a mask on the bird layer to hide the hand.
- Created a selection of the bird and branch using the **Select Subject** tool and output this as a new layer with a mask.
- Imported the Midjourney abstract background and positioned this layer below the bird layer. Used the **Transform** tool to adjust the position of the colored background. Adjusted the mask using white and black brushes to ensure there was no halo around the bird.
- Applied a **Harmonization Neural Filter** to match the color temperature and tone of the bird and branch to the background.

I have used the same approach to create a wide variety of "painterly" images, where I merge bird or animal photos that I have taken with my camera, with abstract backgrounds created in Midjourney. If you don't happen to be a bird photographer, you can also create both the bird image and background in Midjourney.

FIGURE 8.10
Examples of my bird photographs composited with abstract backgrounds.
©Julie Pallant

Photoshop can also be a useful tool if you wish to produce your AI images as greeting cards. I have created a Photoshop template which includes the image on the front of the card and my business name and contact details on the back (when folded). I can use this template multiple times, just by swapping out the image layers.

These templates are sized so that I can print two images on an A4 piece of matte photo paper – this makes the printing very cost effective.

I print my cards on my Canon Pro-300 printer but if you don't have your own printer, you can send the file off to a commercial printing company.

Figure 8.11 Card template created in Photoshop.

Programs to Enlarge Your Images for Printing

The images that are output from Midjourney are relatively small, and while this makes them ideal for using online, they may not be suitable for printing as wall art, prints, or canvases. If you want to obtain high-quality prints of an upscaled Midjourney image any larger than 6.8 inches (17.27 cm) you will need to use a program to increase the number of pixels in your image. The program that I use and recommend is **Topaz Gigapixel AI**. Before I demonstrate how to use the program, there is a bit of background theory and terminology that you might find helpful first or alternatively you can access the same tool in Topaz Photo AI.

Calculating the Required Image Size

The original generated image in Midjourney is currently a square 1024 × 1024 pixels. After upscaling in Midjourney this doubles to 2048 × 2048 pixels at 72 pixels per inch. Ideally, images for printing should be 300 pixels per inch to ensure sharper images with finer details, although you can get away with values lower than this, particularly if your print will be viewed from a distance.

To calculate how big you could print a Midjourney image, you divide the number of pixels (2048) by the desired pixels per inch value (300):

2048/300 = 6.8 inches (or 17.27 cm)

So, if you want to ensure a high-quality print, you can only print your upscaled Midjourney image up to the size of 6.8 inches (17.27 cm). If you go much larger than this, you may see pixelation and your image could appear fuzzy and lacking detail when viewed up close. However, if you intend your image to be viewed from a considerable distance away (e.g., billboard or banner), you can use much lower values than the recommended 300 ppi.

The other way to approach this issue is to think about what size you want your printed image to be. This is important if you are intending to sell your images or to upload them to a print-on-demand site.

In the example below, I demonstrate how to work out the pixel size needed for an image which has an aspect ratio of 3:2 that you want to print at 30 inches × 20 inches (76.2 × 50.8 cm) with the high quality of 300 dpi.

The formula is:

Intended print Width in inches × 300 = number of pixels for the width
Intended print Height in inches × 300 = number of pixels for the height

Using this formula, our calculation for a 30 inches × 20 inches print is:

Width: 30 × 300 = 9000 px
Height: 20 × 300 = 6000 px

The result of this calculation indicates that, in order to print my image at 30 inches × 20 inches, I need to increase my pixels to 9000 px × 6000 px. I can now use this information in Topaz Gigapixel to upsize my image. Details of this program are provided in the next section.

For a very detailed and in-depth review of upscaling images from print, you can check out the YouTube video below:

Ey-Eye (2024). How to upscale Midjourney images for print – all you need to know www.youtube.com/watch?v=57kd6CeWU34.

Topaz Gigapixel AI

While there are some free upscaling programs available, I strongly recommend that you consider using Topaz Gigapixel AI if you intend to print your images, or you are providing images to clients or Topaz

Photo AI. In addition to increasing the size of your image suitable for printing, it helps to boost the sharpness and clarity of your images, enhances the details in the image, and helps fix pixelation and other artifacts.

You can purchase Topaz Gigapixel AI from the topazlabs.com site for a one-off payment of US$99.00 (keep an eye out for when it is on sale). It can be used as a stand-alone program, or alternatively, it can be activated from within Adobe Photoshop under the **File – Automate** menu.

One of the advantages of using a program like Topaz Gigapixel AI is that it allows batch processing of multiple images, saving you a lot of time, and speeding up your workflow. This is particularly beneficial if you need to prepare a lot of images to be uploaded to print-on-demand sites for example.

In the example below I demonstrate the steps in Topaz Gigapixel AI to upsize this image of an owl I created in Midjourney.

Step 1: Check the size of the image in Photoshop

Opened the image in Photoshop and checked the size of the image by going up to the **Image** menu on the top left of the screen and choosing **Image Size**.

Figure 8.12 Midjourney image of an owl.

Checked that the **Resample** button is NOT ticked.

Changed the **Resolution** value from 72 to **300**.

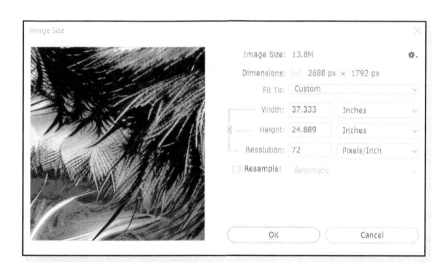

This screen shows that the image is currently 2688 px × 1792 px. To print the image at high quality (300 dpi), it tells me I should not exceed 8.96 inches × 5.973 inches.

If I want to print it as a 30 inches × 20 inches quality print, our earlier calculations suggest I will need to increase the size of the image to 9000 px × 6000 px. I will use this information in the Topaz Gigapixel AI program.

Step 2: Open the Gigapixel AI Plugin in Photoshop

After downloading and installing Topaz Gigapixel it can be accessed in Photoshop by going up to the **File** menu at the top left of the screen and choosing **Automate**. In the pop-out menu, I clicked on **Topaz Gigapixel AI Plugin**.

Step 3: Select the AI model and desired size of the upscale image

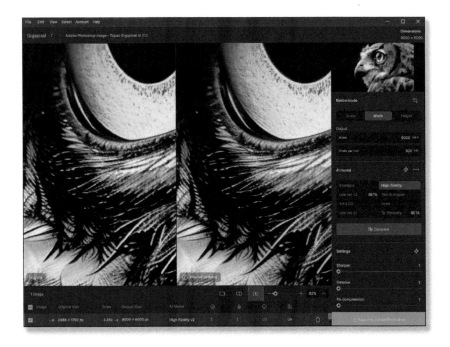

In the Topaz Gigapixel AI window, I set the **Resize mode** to **Width** and changed the width of the image in the **Output** section to 9000 px.

I checked that the **Pixels per inch** value was 300 ppi.

If you prefer, you can resize it by using the **Scale** button by asking for a 2×, 4×, or 6× increase in the image.

There are a number of individual AI models you can choose from, or you can press the **Compare** button and view the different models in a grid. Experiment to see which one works best with your image. For photographic images, I tend to use **Standard** or **High Fidelity** models. For upsizing screenshots or other text-based images, I use the **Text and Shapes** model.

Once you have selected your size and model this information will appear in a summary box along the bottom of the Topaz Gigapixel AI window.

In this example I asked the program to increase my image from the **Original Size** of 2688 × 1792 px to an **Output Size** of 9000 × 6000 px using the **High Fidelity** AI model. My selections are shown on the bottom of the screen of the Gigapixel window.

To activate, I pressed the blue button **Export to Adobe Photoshop**. The process takes a few minutes and the upsized image will appear in the main window of Photoshop as an extra layer in the layer stack. The file can be saved as a TIFF or PSD file if further editing is needed, or exported as a JPG.

For a very detailed comparison of Topaz Gigapixel AI against other upscaler programs you might like to go to: https://midlibrary.io/midguide/upscaling-ai-art-for-printing. On this site, there is also a library of art styles you might want to try out (these are discussed in more detail in the Resources for Artists section).

Resources for Photographers

YouTube is a great resource for photographers looking for examples of how Midjourney can be used as a creative tool in a photographic workflow. For product and food photographers there are some great videos showing how to create AI backgrounds, elements, and props that can save you a lot of time and money.

There are many more photographers embracing AI as a tool and taking advantage of this hybrid approach to image creation. Martin Botvidsson is a product photographer who uses AI as a very effective part of his workflow. According to the introduction to one of his videos (*AI for Photographers: Your Design Buddy Midjourney*):

> Discover the game-changing fusion of photography and AI In this video, I explore how photographers can elevate their business by integrating AI to create stunning art illustrations and combine it with their photographs.
>
> *Botvidsson: www.youtube.com/watch?v=2ZW8MhuSeUg*

As a photographer myself I really like the fact that he demonstrates all the steps in the process, from taking the photographic images in the studio, and then merging them in Photoshop with backgrounds created in Midjourney.

Botvidsson has other videos where he collaborates with Oliver Fox, an Austrian food and product photographer to create different backgrounds in Midjourney for images of gin bottles. In a series of three videos, they demonstrate how they use Midjourney to create the background, shoot the bottles of gin, and then merge the AI and photographic elements.

In the first video in this series (www.youtube.com/watch?v=fQG5wVTE-DE) Botvidsson and Fox demonstrate the process they use to create a forest background image in Midjourney – this provides a great example of the creative process in action as they generate, refine, and regenerate images until they get the one that suits their purpose. The video was shot in 2023, so they use the older Discord version of Midjourney, but the same steps are relevant if you are using the current online platform.

In the third video in the series Botvidsson demonstrates how he uses Photoshop to combine the background and the photograph of the real gin bottle. This is a great opportunity to improve your knowledge and skills in using Photoshop.

There is another example in the first video that you might find useful. Oliver Fox describes his hybrid approach, where he uses Midjourney to create an image of a bottle of gin on a table surrounded by glasses, and then uses Photoshop to replace the AI bottle with a photograph he took of the real bottle. He explains that, when writing the Midjourney prompt, he describes in great detail the setup that he wants, including the bottle and the lighting.

To achieve the Midjourney images Oliver specified, as part of the prompt, that he wanted a "red liqueur bottle with back lighting". Midjourney then creates the appropriate bottle shadows and reflections in the image. Oliver uses this AI-generated image to guide the lighting setup when shooting the real bottle in the studio. In post-production, he then swaps out the Midjourney bottle with the real one using Photoshop.

Both Oliver and Botvidsson emphasize the need to experiment with the prompts, tweaking as necessary, to achieve the final result. They warn that this can take some time, starting with simple prompts and adding extra descriptive words and details to guide Midjourney.

Resources for Artists

The growth of AI is likely to have a big impact on both traditional and digital artists. According to an article on the https//worklife.vc/blog/ai-artist (February 22, 2023) website: "Artistic industries are experiencing one of the most significant disruptions in centuries with the meteoric rise of AI tools for art". They go on to conclude: "The debate around AI-generated art is far from over, but one thing is clear: this technology is here to stay. So, whether you're a traditionalist or a tech enthusiast, there's no denying the potential of AI to revolutionize the art world".

If you are an artist and looking for inspiration on how to utilize AI a website to check out is AIArtists. org – they claim to be the "the world's largest community of artists exploring Artificial Intelligence". This site features the work of a wide range of different artists who use AI as part of their work. It also has a list of resources that you might find useful.

One very helpful resource if you are interested in exploring different art styles and applying them to your Midjourney images is Andrei Kovalev's Midlibrary: Midjourney AI Styles Library and Guide (https://midlibrary.io/). This site catalogs an enormous range of different artists and art styles with over 52,000 images, showing 4970 styles broken into categories (e.g. photographers, painters, fashion designers, illustrators, and art movements) and classified according to themes, color schemes, subjects, and artistic techniques.

Midlibrary is a great resource if you are searching for a particular style of image, or if you want some inspiration to give your image a different look. This site includes examples from different art movements and eras (Art Nouveau, Surrealism, Folk Art, and Impressionism), and specific artists and photographers.

If you would like to apply one of the styles shown on the site to your own image, go to the Midjourney prompt box and type the word **By** followed by the name of the art style and then a description of the image that you want.

So, if I wanted an image of a young woman in the style of Art Nouveau I could type: **By Art Nouveau, young woman**

Alternatively, you can use the prompt structure: **young woman in the style of Art Nouveau**.

You might like to experiment to see which approach gives the best results for you.

Prompt: By Art Nouveau, young woman

FIGURE 8.13
Example of an Midjourney image inspired by Art Nouveau.

You won't get the same image as shown in the example on the Midlibrary site. Midjourney will apply the art medium (watercolor, oil, and line drawing) and art style color palette to the subject you have requested.

The art style you choose can have quite a dramatic effect on the results. In the example below I used a simple prompt (young woman) and applied a variety of different styles. Obviously, when using this approach yourself you can write far more complex prompts, telling Midjourney exactly what you want included in the image.

FIGURE 8.14
Examples of different art styles.

On the Midlibrary site you can see examples of images generated using specific artist's/designer's names in the prompts. Before specifying these artists' names in your own prompts, you might like to consider how you feel about the ethics of using prompts containing the names of artists who are still living and trying to earn a living from their art.

There are many of us who are generating AI images that feel uncomfortable about copying a living artist's work, particularly if we intend to use the images commercially. I always check on Wikipedia to see whether the artist is still alive. One way that you can avoid directly replicating an artist's style is to combine two or more artists in one prompt – this can sometimes result in some totally unique images.

I have included examples below of images created by specifying an artist's name in the prompt, along with my text prompt "young woman". Obviously when you are creating your own prompts you would include much more detail about what you wanted in your image.

Please note: none of the artists used in the prompts in Figure 8.15 are still living.

FIGURE 8.15
Examples of images created by specifying an artist's name.

Another resource you might find helpful is a set of YouTube videos by Making AI Magic (real name: Jenn Mishra), where she reviews a wide range of different art styles. She describes each of the art styles with very creative examples. Be prepared to experiment, you might be surprised with the results.

Resources for Designers

A recent article on the Worklife site (www.worklife.vc/blog/ai-artist) explores a variety of creative uses of AI for designers. This includes designing buildings, architecture, furniture, and interior design, fashion, jewelry, nails, and makeup.

The article features the work of Manas Bhatia, an architect who utilizes AI "as another tool that can enrich the design process and spark new ideas, … . he envisions a future where AI is integrated into the software architects use to model their visions" (Worklife, 2023). If building design is an area that interests you check out an article on Manas Bhatia's fantasy building structures built around nature themes in the My Modern Met article "Architect uses AI to create utopia where buildings grow and breathe" (Stewart, 2022).

Manas Bhatia's Instagram site (@manasbhatiadesign/) features a range of very organic buildings and interior designs all created with Midjourney. For lots more ideas on the applications of AI in architecture you could also try searching by the Instagram hashtags #midjourneyarchitecture and #aiarchitecture.

If you are interested in how AI image generators could be used in architectural design there is a great series of YouTube videos by Eric Reinholdt using the site name of *30 × 40 Design Workshop*. In his video "Using AI as a design tool in my architecture practice" he demonstrates various ways he uses Midjourney in the design process. His Instagram site @30by40 has over 100,000 followers.

Interior design is another area that has embraced the use of AI to stimulate creativity and explore possibilities. You can see examples of this on Instagram using the hashtag #aiinteriordesign. You might also get some ideas for prompts that you can use from the **Explore** section of Midjourney.

I have included a few examples in Figure 8.16 of furniture design images that I generated by adapting prompts that I found on the **Explore** gallery. There is an enormous range of possibilities – it is just a matter of playing with your prompt to customize it to your needs.

Prompt: Design for a futuristic office chair

Prompt: wooden table with beautiful curving legs

Prompt: skateboard-shaped coffee table made of wood, leather and glass

FIGURE 8.16
Examples of furniture designs created in Midjourney.

I am not sure how practical or comfortable some of the designs that Midjourney creates will be, but as a source of inspiration and ideas, they are an interesting place to start.

Midjourney is also a useful tool for exploring combinations of colors to be used in interior design – certainly a lot cheaper than buying numerous paint samples! In the examples shown in Figure 8.17 I asked Midjourney to create different color palettes, adjusting the wording of the prompt to suit.

Prompt: a warm, earthy colour palette of 6 colour swatches for interior design

Prompt: Bright and fresh spring colors such as mint green, soft pink, sunny yellow and peach.

Prompt: a colorful fun interior, vivid colors, maroon, orange, teal, purple, pink, bright, fun playful

FIGURE 8.17
Examples of color palettes.

The ability to explore color schemes is also a useful feature of Midjourney for web designers and content creators. In the **Explore** gallery of Midjourney, if you type: *color scheme web* into the search box you will get different ideas for color combinations to suit different purposes. This is a great way to learn how to craft a prompt to communicate your ideas.

Prompt: a color scheme for a website about spiritualism, healing, modern, friendly, calm

Prompt: color palette for a tech start-up website

Prompt: Color palette using colors Gumtree Grey, Waratah Red, Acacia Green, Sunrise Pink

FIGURE 8.18
Examples of color schemes.

By changing your prompt, you can also ask to see website layouts showing the colors used in the design. These are useful as mood boards to show clients so they can explore the overall look and feel of a design before you actually start creating the website. I have included a few examples from the **Explore** gallery in Figure 8.19.

Prompt: Website for a business specializing in decoration services. Landing page design, minimalistic Colors: warm, not very bright. Pastel colors like pink and peach.

Prompt: Web design for a university, modern, white, electric blue and neon green colours

Prompt: Portfolio website design for a digital media business, with images of photography production set, red and black color scheme

FIGURE 8.19
Examples of website designs.

Fashion designers have embraced AI as a way of quickly generating varied and detailed images, speeding up the creative process, and sparking innovation. Midjourney gives you the flexibility to explore a range of diverse styles and aesthetics, broadening the creative possibilities in a cost-effective way.

One very colorful example of a fashion designer using AI tools is the Instagram site of Salome Castro.

FIGURE 8.20
AI fashion images created by Salome Castro.
@salomeillustrates: Images used with permission of the artist

Another Instagram site with some interesting ideas for fashion, hairstyles, make up and props is: ai_fashion_photos, a digital creator with over 97,000 followers. Her work was featured in the first ever AI fashion week held in April 2023, which showcased the AI-generated work of over 400 creatives from around the world. In an interview with the *New York Post* (DeNinno, 2023), Fran, the creator of these images revealed that she is a civil rights lawyer, having previously worked as a photographer, who creates AI-fashion images as a hobby.

Midjourney is a great tool that allows makeup artists to experiment with bold, innovative concepts without the cost of physical creation – instead clients can be provided with a digital preview of potential looks. If you are a makeup artist searching for ideas for some more creative designs, you might like to type: *makeup designs* into the search box under the **Explore** section of Midjourney. Here you will find a wide range of different designs that other users have created.

I have included a few of the more dramatic looks I was able to generate in Figure 8.21.

Prompt: a glamour up-to-date color palette for a pop singer

Prompt: Portrait photo of a girl with Chinese dragon pattern drawn on her face with makeup, bold shapes, black intricate color palette, Chinese New Year, high saturation

Prompt: 30-year-old woman facing the camera, futuristic makeup, high fashion studio photography, gray backdrop

FIGURE 8.21
Examples of fashion makeup images generated in Midjourney.

If you are a nail artist, you can use Midjourney in the same way to generate innovative nail designs to showcase to clients. By inputting specific prompts that describe desired colors, patterns, or themes, you can quickly and easily receive a variety of unique, eye-catching designs. This not only enhances your creativity, but also provides clients with a preview of how different designs might look before application.

Here are some of the images that I found on **Explore** by typing *fingernail art* into the search bar.

FIGURE 8.22
Examples of fingernail art designs.

A search of **Explore** using the words **jewelry design** revealed an amazing range of designs for rings, necklaces, and earrings – great ideas to inspire unique, and very creative pieces. Copy the prompt of any of the designs you like and add or subtract words to tweak it to suit your needs. You may also find these images a useful guide when creating a display to promote or sell your products.

Midjourney creator: xelalexela

Midjourney creator: Glorious_papaya_66566

Midjourney creator: Lyuda64

FIGURE 8.23
Examples of jewelry designs.

Midjourney is also an ideal tool for tattoo artists wanting to prepare a booklet of designs for their clients to choose from. By varying the prompt, you can create designs for males and females, across a variety of themes, or featuring specific objects or elements. To further customize the design, you could work with the client in Midjourney to produce a unique, one-off design that is meaningful for them.

To see some examples of prompts that other people have used, type in *tattoo designs* into the **Explore** gallery in Midjourney and add additional words (e.g. butterfly, skull, bird, etc.) to refine the selection. When you search for tattoo designs, you will sometimes get black and white line drawings, and at other times Midjourney will show the design on a person. I have included some examples with their prompts in Figure 8.24.

Prompt: Gothic tattoo vector, simple shapes, no shadow, white background

Prompt: Black and white tattoo, Illustration of wolf, low detail, thick lines, no shading

Prompt: A refined black and white tattoo art of butterflies, delicate fine line pen work, detailed wings, minimalist, high-quality, on a stark white background

Prompt: a Celtic style line art tattoo of a raven on a powerful Viking warrior's back

Prompt: horizontal back tattoo, flowers, butterflies, colorful, feathers

Prompt: Viking dragon tattoo sleeve design for men

FIGURE 8.24
Examples of tattoo designs.

References

DeNinno, N. (2023, April 20). First-ever AI fashion week debuts in NYC: 'A new realm of creation'. *New York Post.* https://nypost.com/2023/04/20/first-ai-fashion-week-coming-to-nyc-new-realm-of-creation

Stewart, J. (2022, 5 November). Architect uses AI to create utopia where buildings grow and breathe. *My Modern Met.* https://mymodernmet.com/manas-bhatia-ai-concept-architecture

Worklife Editorial. (2023, 22 February). Artistic industries are experiencing one of the most significant disruptions in centuries with the meteoric rise of AI tools for art. *Worklife Blog.* https://worklife.vc/blog/ai-artist

9

Conclusion

My aim in writing this book was to introduce you to this amazing program Midjourney and to provide an easy-to-follow guide to all that it offers. Throughout the chapters in this book, you've learned about the extensive capabilities of Midjourney, an AI-powered image generation platform that is a valuable asset for a wide variety of different professions. As you've seen from the examples and techniques covered, Midjourney is a powerful and flexible tool that has the potential to revolutionize the way we approach image creation.

Throughout this book, I have taken you step-by-step through the process of using Midjourney to generate different types of images, and demonstrated just how versatile and adaptable this tool can be. From photographers, artists and designers to marketers and educators, Midjourney's applications are many and varied. Whether you're looking to create eye catching artwork, enhance your marketing materials, or simply explore your creativity, Midjourney has something to offer. Its ability to generate high-quality images quickly and easily makes it an invaluable resource for anyone looking to bring their ideas to life.

Your success with Midjourney will largely depend on how effectively you can craft prompts. The quality of your prompts directly influences the quality and suitability of the output that you obtain. Use the various tools I have provided throughout the book to learn as much as you can about the art of "promptology". I encourage you to take full advantage of the opportunity that the community-based philosophy of Midjourney provides to learn from the many millions of other users of the program.

It is crucial to be patient and willing to refine your prompts based on the initial results. Very rarely will you get the exact image that you want on the first try. Take an experimental approach trying different terms, descriptions, and art styles. This iterative process is key to achieving the best possible images from Midjourney.

Midjourney is constantly evolving, with new features and updates being added all the time. To get the most out of this tool, it is important to stay up to date with the latest developments and to experiment with new techniques and tools as they become available. By doing so, you'll be able to tap into the full potential of Midjourney and benefit from what the platform has to offer, now and into the future. Embrace the opportunity to experiment with its capabilities and integrate this advanced technology into your workflow. Let Midjourney be a partner in your creative endeavors, whatever they might be.

So, as you close this book, remember that the possibilities with Midjourney are endless. Don't be afraid to explore, experiment, and push the boundaries of what's possible. Share your creations with others and learn from their experiences. And most importantly, keep practicing and honing your skills – with Midjourney, the more you use it, the more you'll discover its full potential. I hope you enjoy the creative process as much as I (and millions of others) have – be warned it can be addictive!

DOI: 10.1201/9781003541677-9

Appendix

Summary Sheet

Generate an image in Create

Click the **Create** button, type the prompt in the prompt box. Open the **Settings** and choose your preferred options.

- **Image size:** choose the shape (**Portrait, Square, Landscape**) and change the aspect ratio using the slider
- **Model:** choose **Standard** to apply Midjourney style or **Raw** to reduce the amount of Midjourney style applied
- **Version:** select the latest version to access all features, V 5.2 for more artistic effects, or **Niji** for anime style
- **Stylization:** adjust to determine amount of Midjourney style is applied (0–1000, 100 = default)
- **Weirdness:** adjust to determine how weird the images are (0–3000)
- **Variety:** adjust to determine how different the four images generated will be (0–100)
- **Speed:** If you have a Standard, Pro, or Mega plan you can generate an unlimited number of images in **Relax mode** but **Fast** hours are limited according to subscription plan.
- **Stealth**: In the Pro and above subscription plans you can choose **Stealth** to hide your images from being seen on the **Explore** gallery.

Details to include in your prompt

- **Medium**: photograph, painting, line drawing, sketch, watercolor, illustration, poster, cartoon, comic book
- **Style**: art style, name of artist, technique
- **Composition**: wide-angle, close-up, overhead, head and shoulders, full body, low angle, eye-level
- **Scene**: subject, location, environment, lighting
- **Modulate**: bright, colorful, energetic, happy, spiritual, dark, dramatic, sinister, mysterious

To include **text** in your image: include words in quotation marks " " e.g. "**Happy New Year**"

Modify a generated image in Create

- Upsize the image: click the **Upscale – Subtle** or **Upscale – Creative**
- Create variations of a generated image: click **Vary – Subtle** or **Vary – Strong**
- Use the **Editor** button to change the aspect ratio, zoom out, modify the prompt or change specific areas of the image
- **Create folders and filters in Organize module**

- **Create a new folder**: select **Organize module**, press the **Organize** button on the top right, open the **Folder** section, and click **Create Folder**
- **Filter images**: select **Organize**, press the **Organize** button on the top right, open the **Filters** section, and choose one of the options to filter by: **Rating, Type, Image Size, or Version**
- Change the way images are displayed in **Organize** module: select **Organize module**, press the **Organize** button on the top right, open the **View Options** section, and click **Layout** or **Image size**

Optional extra commands to be added to the end of a prompt

Aspect ratio: changes the shape of the image

    --ar 2:3 or --ar 16:9 first number is the width, second is the height

Version: changes which version of the program is used

    --v 6, --v 5.2, --niji 6

Stylization: determines how much Midjourney's default style is applied

    --stylize 100 (can be shortened to **--s**) Range: 0–1000, low = 50, medium = 100, high = 250, very high = 750

Variety: determines how much variability there will be among the four images generated

    --c 100 Range: 0–100, high values produce more variation

Specifying elements not to be included:

    --no people, cars separate each of the elements to be excluded with a comma

Image weights: used to indicate how important an image should be in the prompt

    --iw 2 Range: 0.5–3 (for Version 6), 0.5–2 (for Version 5)

Style reference: used to indicate how much the style of an image prompt is applied

    --sw 100 Range: 0–1000, default = 100

Character weight: determines how much of the character in the reference image is included

    --cw 0 The face will be replicated, but not the clothes or accessories

    Range: 0–100, higher values will retain more of the original character reference image details

Tile: to create a design that can be repeated to form a continuous pattern

    --tile

Permutations: run multiple generations within the single prompt

    photograph of cute {puppy, kitten} sitting in a box Enclose the variations within curly brackets { }. Permissible number depends on your subscription: basic = 4, standard = 10, Pro and Mega = 40

Repeat: specifies the number of times to rerun the prompt to generate more images

    --repeat 5 (can be shortened to **--r**) Range 0–10 (for Basic or Standard plans) and 0–30 (Pro or Mega plans)

Additional resources

Manage your Subscription plan and Billing details: click your username at the bottom left of the screen

- Change the color of the Midjourney screen: toggle between **Dark Mode** and **Light Mode** on the bottom left of the screen
- Report problems with the program: click on **Report Bug** button
- Get help with Billing issues: click on **Help** and choose **Billing Support**
- Access the Midjourney Documentation: click on **Help** and choose **Getting Started**
- Get updates on recent changes to the program: click on the **Updates** icon

View other user's images

- Click on the **Explore** button and choose **Random, Hot, Top Day,** or **Likes**
- Click on an image to enlarge it
- To use the prompt of an image in the **Explore** gallery click on the **Prompt** button on the bottom right of the screen
- To use an image from **Explore** in your own prompt click on the **Image** button on the bottom right of the screen
- To copy the style of an image click on the **Style** button on the bottom right of the screen

Index

Note: the **bold** items refer to a specific tool or feature in Midjourney.